EXTEND
YOUR HOME

EXTEND YOUR HOME

amanda katz

Acknowledgements

Written by and based on designs by Amanda Katz Architect;
illustrations by Fergus Duncan and Jac van Ryswyk;
computer drawings by Mike Rodseth and John Alves;
initial planning assistance from Robert de Jager Architect;
general assistance and input from Paul Duncan;
input regarding Council approval of plans
from C Du Preez: building control officer, Cape Town.

Struik Publishers (Pty) Ltd
(A member of The Struik Publishing Group (Pty) Ltd)
Cornelis Struik House, 80 McKenzie Street
Cape Town 8001

Reg. No. 54/00965/07

First published by Struik Publishers (Pty) Ltd 1998

Published edition © Struik Publishers 1998
Text © Amanda Katz 1998
Illustrations © Amanda Katz 1998

Editor: Hilda Hermann
Designer: Dominic Robson
Cover designer: Petal Palmer
Illustrators: Fergus Duncan, Jac van Ryswyk
Proofreader: Sally Dicey

Set by Struik DTP, Cape Town
Reproduction by Hirt & Carter Pty (Ltd), Cape Town
Printed and bound by CTP, Cape Town

ISBN 1 86872 084 5

Also available in Afrikaans as
Vergroot Jou Huis

CONTENTS

INTRODUCTION

This book shows you the potential your home has for remodelling and extension. An enlightened client is the best possible partner for an able and sympathetic architect or designer. Instead of being a stressful experience, where you watch your home crumbling around you, extending and improving your home should, and indeed can, be exciting and rewarding. The final result should be a domestic environment tailored precisely to your needs, your taste and your style of living.

YOUR REQUIREMENTS

Over time, your home requirements will inevitably change; what was ideal when you first moved in may be far from practical a few years later. Families grow, friends move on, financial circumstances change, ways of life alter. When children are young, one has to consider where they are going to play and, when they're older, where they may entertain their friends. Most parents need privacy and a place to call their own. At a later stage, children leave home and grandparents may move in. Lifestyles change – for example, you may choose, or need, to work from home.

These are just some of the factors that should be taken into consideration when you plan to increase the size of your home or remodel rooms. Ideally the spaces should be adaptable for different purposes as your needs change.

LIKES AND DISLIKES

How do you know what is right for you and the best ways to achieve your goals?

If you have lived in your home for some time you will know the spaces that work for you and the ones that don't suit your household needs. Remember, there is no universal dream home. Your likes and dislikes, what works and what does not, are particular to your environment and to your lifestyle.

EVALUATE WHAT YOU HAVE

Start by evaluating what you have and be clear as to exactly what it is you wish to achieve by improving, remodelling or extending. Only minor adjustments may be needed, such as moving doors or walls to create better flow through the space. You may need to alter or add to create more rooms, in which case physical boundaries such as walls, ceilings and floors will have to be modified. You may want to add on new space – perhaps a new room, a bay window or an extra floor. You will need to look at the structure of the house and the way the roof is constructed to determine the simplicity and cost-effectiveness of the extension.

THE CHARACTER OF YOUR HOME

When extending your home, it is important to consider its existing character. If it has a particularly dominant feature, work with it so that the extension does not look 'added on' and compromise the overall feel. The character of a house is often its best selling point. It is sometimes difficult to define character but, among other things, it has to do with the shape of the roof, the material used for the walls and the type of doors and windows.

You may want to change the character to match the times or to suit maintenance requirements. It is important to be consistent when you extend your home and, if you are planning to change the overall appearance, to ensure that there is a master plan with long-term options which can be effected to ensure that the results will be harmonious.

Good design can sometimes offset different characters and styles with a harmonious result, but this requires the retention of wall-to-opening proportions or a feature of the original house which is carried throughout – for example, a plaster detail, a facebrick plinth or parapet walls. Whatever you decide to do, consider the basic character of your home and that of the street and neighbourhood. Aim to add value to the property, rather than devalue it.

DO IT YOURSELF?

Our intention is that you use this book as a way of finding out what is possible and feasible. We are not suggesting that you design your own alterations and additions. And we do not recommend that you attempt to carry out the building work alone, do-it-yourself-style, unless you have had previous experience or have the time and motivation to do so. (*See* page 15 for the advantages and disadvantages of the DIY approach.)

USE AN ARCHITECT

Whatever your requirements, it will help to talk to an architect or a designer who specialises in this sort of work. Altering and extending your home is very complex and can be expensive if it is not well planned. It can be worrying to attempt an extension on your own and it often helps to consult an architect or trained designer to consolidate your ideas and to make the process enjoyable rather than weighed down with complications. Use an architect or designer with whom you feel comfortable. Their training encompasses not only design work but also legal matters relating to the extension, building code requirements, and the administration and financial control of the actual building works. Architects are trained to guide their clients through the building process. They can often save money for the home owner because a well-thought-out and executed design will increase the resale value of a property. Concentrate on how you wish to live and leave the actual solutions to the architect.

ABOUT THIS BOOK

This book is intended to be a source for ideas and a guide to planning your extension. The ideas are based on my own architectural planning and building efforts over the past ten years. Checklists for planning and budgeting are included and there is a section dealing with legal matters. The extension examples have been divided into five categories:

- remodelling existing space;
- converting unused space;
- adding new space;
- kitchens and bathrooms; and
- minor additions.

There are checklists to help you confirm your requirements and plan your extension. Use them when consolidating your thoughts on planning and design, evaluating what you have and determining what to include in your budget.

The planning and design checklist on page 9 will help you to evaluate what you have. The section on style (*see* page 11) will prompt you to consider how your extension will be linked to the existing building.

A list of the planning stages necessary to ensure that the result suits your needs and budget can be found on page 12. Should you do it yourself or appoint an architect or designer? Consider the pros and cons of each approach on page 13 not to mention the legal aspects of your planning strategy (*see* page 15). This may be the second-largest financial outlay you make after purchasing your home. The potential hazards and areas of conflict and stress which could be avoided with proper planning are also highlighted.

The plans used as examples are of actual completed work designed by architects. An explanation of how to read a drawing and a key to the symbols used on the drawings can be found on pages 19 and 20.

Finally, there is a glossary of frequently used building terms and suggested reading if you decide to 'go it alone'.

It has been assumed by the author that the reader has no previous knowledge of building or architectural practice and the text has been written to allow you to carefully consider the options available when choosing to extend your home.

TEN STEPS TO AN EXTENSION

1 Evaluate what you have.
Source copies of your house plans at your local authority.
Obtain a copy of your property's title deeds from the surveyor general.

2 Confirm your needs. (Use the design and planning checklist on page 9 to help you.)

3 Assess your budget and time. (For guidelines on what to include in your budget see page 12.)

4 Meet with and appoint an architect or designer.

5 The architect will prepare sketch drawings for your approval, based on your needs and budget.

6 Check the feasibility of the plans and check the cost estimate, based on the architect's sketch plans, with a builder or quantity surveyor.

7 The architect will prepare plans and submit these to the local authority for approval.
You may need to appoint a structural engineer if your local authority requires this.

8 The architect will prepare construction drawings and specification of work – called tender drawings – from which three or four builders can prepare accurate quotations.

9 The builders will present their quotations.
Based on your architect's recommendations, confirm which builder you wish to appoint.

10 Draw up and sign a standard building contract with your builder and arrange for your architect to inspect the building work regularly (once or twice a week is considered reasonable).
The architect will check the quality of work and control payments. S/he will ensure that the builder is not overpaid and is paid on time to allow for the smooth running of the site.

PLANNING AND DESIGN CHECKLIST

Several factors will affect how much you do and how much time, effort and money you invest in your home extension. The following planning and design process can help you with this review so that you can determine the nature, scope and feasibility of your home extension. This will help you to clarify your needs and explore specific ways of extending your home to create what you would like to achieve.

LONG-TERM PLANS
- Are you planning to sell or stay in your home?

EVALUATE WHAT YOU HAVE
- What spaces do you already have?
- Do you have a copy of your house plans?

WHAT DO YOU WANT TO ACHIEVE WITH THE PLANNED EXTENSION?
- More bedrooms, bathrooms, a new kitchen, access to the garden?

WHAT ARE YOUR RESOURCES AND LIMITATIONS?
- How much money do you want to spend?
- When does the work need to be completed?
- Are there any building regulations relating to the property?
- Do you want to build the extension yourself or have it built for you?

WHAT ARE YOUR LONG-TERM PLANS?

Are you planning to sell your home or do you hope to keep it for a long time?
If you are planning to sell you need to consider how the cost of the extension will affect the value of your property. If you are planning to stay, meeting your living needs may be more important than the immediate economic return on your home as an investment.

How will you use your home in the future?
Are you planning to have a larger family? Are children moving out? Are elderly parents moving in? Do you want to rent out rooms?

What image or appearance do you want your home to have?
Is your home your private retreat, sheltered from your neighbours and the street, or do you like to entertain friends and keep a sense of openness with your neighbourhood? Do you want your home to be a place to relax, study, raise a family or run a business?

HOW DO YOU EVALUATE AND DOCUMENT WHAT YOU HAVE?

- Source any plans of your property that you may have on file. Alternatively contact your local authority survey branch as plans are usually kept there.
- If there are no plans available, you will need to arrange for your home to be surveyed and the plans will have to be drawn by yourself, an architect or a draftsman. In the early stages of planning, while you are thinking about what you need, it is useful to work with a rough drawing of what you have. This can be checked for accuracy later.
- Consider the structure of your property. What are the walls made of? What sort of roof do you have and where are the supports? Looking inside the existing roof space, if it is accessible, can tell you a lot about how your house is structured.
- Consider your house in relation to your property. How far is it from the boundaries and what are its immediate surroundings (paving, lawn, planting, patios, pergolas, outbuildings, yards, etc.)?
- Consider and note the exterior conditions such as weather (sun, wind and rain direction), views, boundaries (fences, walls, gates, driveways, etc.).

WHAT ARE YOUR WANTS AND NEEDS?

- Functional considerations: efficient use of space, effective circulation, zoning of spaces for privacy or to encourage social gathering.
- Technical considerations: correcting structural problems, repairing deterioration, safety (balustrades and railings at steps, balconies, patios and areas where people could fall), making suitable space for a time when you may be temporarily or permanently disabled.
- Aesthetic considerations: desired appearance, image and style of the house and the interior spaces.
- Your 'gut feel' about your home; what you really like and dislike about it.

WHAT ARE YOUR RESOURCES/LIMITATIONS?

- Available money (budget).
- Available time, skills and materials.
- Zoning, building regulations, and title deed requirements and restrictions.
- Professional assistance: architect, engineer, builder.

Additional considerations include:
- exploring possible design solutions;
- making decisions;
- preparing for construction; and
- starting construction of your home extension.

FACTORS AFFECTING AN EXTENSION

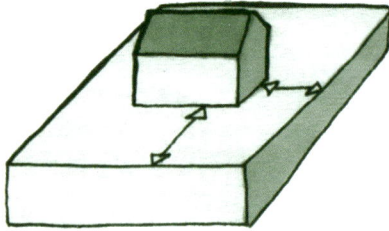

Building position in relation to the property's boundaries.

The position of neighbouring buildings.

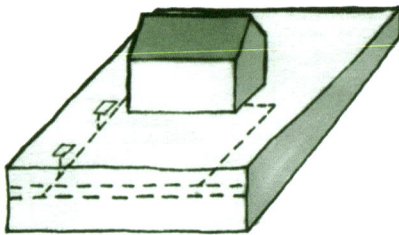

Location of service pipes (electrical cables and sewer runs). These may affect the area where you can extend.

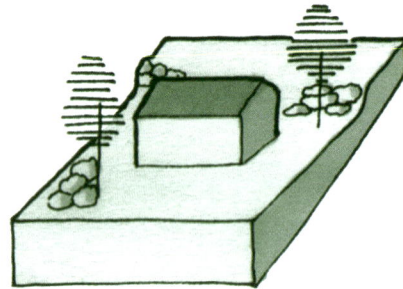

Existing landscaping: special trees, plants or water features that you want to retain.

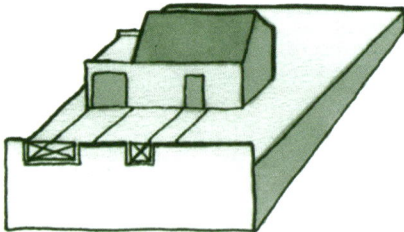

Access from the street for pedestrians and cars

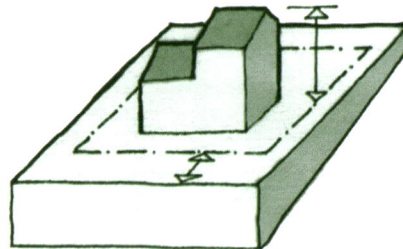

Building and town planning regulations related to your property. Ask your architect or a building inspector at your local authority where plans are approved about these factors.

The effects of weather on your home. For example, from which direction does the wind and rain come and where are the sunny places located?

Views you want to maintain or create.

CAPE DUTCH

VICTORIAN

COTTAGE

MODERN

SETTLER

CORRUGATED-IRON
COTTAGE

SPANISH

FLAT ROOF
DWELLING

STYLE AND CONTEXT

CONSIDER YOUR NEIGHBOURS

If you live on a smallholding or in an average modern suburb where the character of the surrounding buildings is inconsistent, you are, in a sense, free to build in any way that suits you. However, if your property is situated in a historically rich or densely urban context, where the character of the houses is consistent, the extension should be designed to fit in and to preserve the character of the area.

- Extend your home with a sense of good neighbourliness.
- Try to avoid blocking out a neighbour's view and sun.
- Improve the general appearance of the street by either planting trees, building an attractive front wall, erecting a fence or planting a hedge. Create an appropriate car and pedestrian entrance if your extension includes these changes or additions.

DON'T DEVALUE YOUR HOME

The style of your home gives it its unique character. The consideration given to this aspect of the design is almost as important as the actual use of the spaces. You may devalue your precious home by making extensions which clash with or destroy its original character or that of the neighbourhood. Confirm the following characteristics of your home:

- *Size and arrangement of the rooms:* small rooms on either side of a central passage, large rooms on one side of a passage, walk-through spaces.
- *Roof:* pitched or flat, parapet walls, large overhanging eaves or no overhang, gable walls, hipped ends.
- *Windows and doors (material and style):* small pane timber, sliding sash windows, sliding doors, French doors, metal or aluminium doors and windows.
- *Wall finish:* plaster and paint, bagged brickwork, facebrick, plastered with a facebrick plinth, timber clad.
- *Proportion:* consider the relationship between wall and opening, roof and wall, and the size and feel of your home related to the proposed extension.

PROPORTION, SCALE AND SIZE

Think about the scale and style of your existing house and, where possible, maintain this in your extension. For example, is your house a single- or double-storey? Does it have large or small windows? What style are the windows and the doors? Think about your street frontage, the height of walls, railings, types of gates, garage entrances, driveways, and space for cars. Think about the way your home is positioned in relation to its side boundaries and neighbouring homes. Is it semi-detached or free-standing? Are there outbuildings at the side or back of your house? How much space is there around your house for extensions? Is this enough for what you are planning? If you intend using the space around your home, where is the best place to locate the extension related to the interior plan? What about the climate? Access to the garden? Space for children to play?

CHANGING THE APPEARANCE OF YOUR HOME

Changing the appearance of your home usually involves expenses that cannot be quantified in square metres gained, but may be valuable in terms of appeal. Sometimes it is a good idea to remove inappropriate extensions to your home to regain its original style and to upgrade its value. For example, it may be that a beautiful, old Victorian home has had its *broekielace* removed and the balconies enclosed. The typical vertical sash windows may have been changed to horizontal-looking steel windows.

STYLE BEFORE

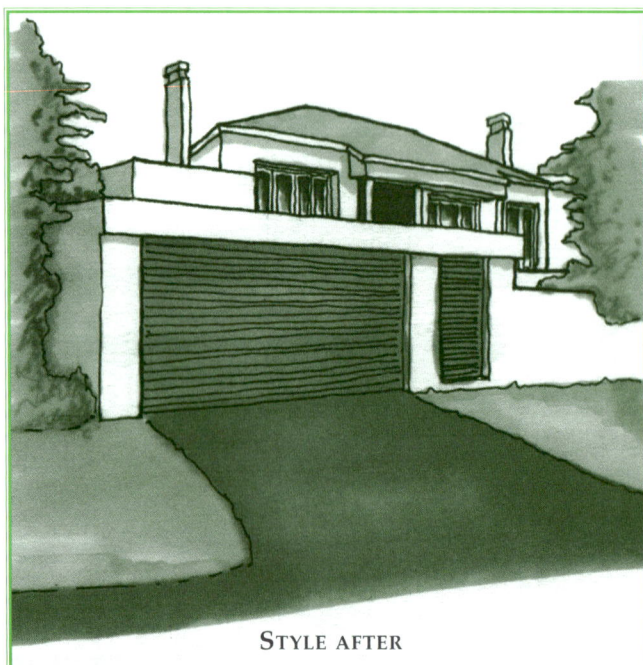

STYLE AFTER

YOUR BUDGET

It usually costs more to build an extension than to build a new home, because existing structures will need to be altered. Your budget for building an extension must include the following costs:

COSTS FOR HAVING PLANS DRAWN

Architects charge an hourly rate or a percentage of the cost of the building work. The services offered by an architect include the preparation of sketch plans, council submission drawings, construction drawings and specification writing, assisting with the selection of a builder, drawing up tender documents, and on-site inspections. Alternatively, you may want to consult an architect on an hourly basis and ask a draftsman to draw the plans.

LOCAL AUTHORITY APPROVAL OF PLANS

The council submission and approval fees are based on the scale and scope of work, and are assessed by the council when the plans are submitted. These fees are not negotiable and may include amounts for waivers to approve sections which do not form part of the building or town planning regulations. The council may call for details from a structural engineer for the structural aspects of your extension or a land surveyor's certificate if the building work is to take place on your site boundary.

ACTUAL COST OF BUILDING

Ask at least three builders to give you quotations for the proposed work as prices vary. Negotiating a cost with one builder for labour-only costs, with you supplying materials, may be a cheaper option but is not recommended, as co-ordinating labour and materials is both difficult and time-consuming.

CONTINGENCIES

Allow an additional 10 to 12% of the building quote for unanticipated problems and additional items required on site once the building work has started

INSURANCE

Inform your insurance brokers that you are doing extensions to your home and ask their advice. The builder usually will insure for items that are not yet built-in (bricks, etc.) whereas you will need to insure any items that are already built or fixed.

SITE SUPERVISION

It is wise to ask your architect to inspect the building work on a regular basis and to control and co-ordinate the project's finances.

FURNISHINGS

Do not forget to make allowances in your budget for items such as light fittings, tiles, carpets, curtains, furniture and built-in cupboards.

USING PROFESSIONALS vs DOING IT YOURSELF

Deciding whether or not to use a professional depends on many factors including: your finance, timing and the desire to learn about and control the creation of your environment. Using professionals (architects and builders) is not more expensive than doing it yourself as the professionals' training and experience should save both time and money.

WORKING WITH PROFESSIONALS

Design and construction co-ordinated by an architect should be of a high quality and completed within both budget and the allotted time. Extending your home is a complex process and it will help to work with an architect specialising in home extensions.

Advice on the pitfalls of extending your home could save you a lot of stress, time and money, and allow you to enjoy the process. There are as many different approaches to the art of building as there are personalities, so choose your architect and builder carefully. They will have different approaches, charge varying fees and respond to your questions in different ways.

What does an architect do?
- S/he helps you to save money by avoiding costly mistakes you may make through ignorance.
- S/he helps you organise your ideas into a workable design that is suited to your budget.
- S/he offers ideas and advice on your home-related needs.
- S/he acts as your agent when dealing with the builder.

The full architectural service includes:
- Preparing drawings for your approval.
- Preparing drawings for submission to the local authority for approval.
- Preparing construction drawings and specifications from which builders can prepare accurate quotations.
- Recommending builders.
- Assistance in signing a standard building contract.
- Administering the building site and regular site meetings (usually one or two per week) to inspect the quality of the building work and to assess the costs to be paid to the builder. Architects do not supervise builders' work and if more thorough supervision is required the owner may employ a project manager.
- Certifying when the building work is complete.

Choosing an architect
- Talk to friends who have worked with architects and builders. Find out from them about the services they offered and whether they would be suited to your needs; or
- Contact your nearest branch of the Institute of Architects and ask for a list of recommended architects specialising in home extensions.

- Look at samples of the work completed by the architect whom you wish to appoint and see if it appeals to you.
- Do not use an architect who disregards your needs, preferences and budget.

Working with an architect
In the beginning it helps to do the following exercises and present the results to your architect so that s/he understands your expectations:

- Compile a list of your needs and wants and let your architect work out how to meet them.
- Collect a scrapbook of photographs and ideas that you like and dislike.
- Be prepared to be honest about your budget and what you can afford to spend.
- Ask your architect to confirm the fees and the way s/he works so that you can budget accordingly.
- Get a written contract stating the services offered, how and when payments need to be made and any anticipated additional expenses.

Architect fees
An architect's fees are based on recommendations by the Institute of Architects and regulated by the *Government Gazette*. However, they may charge what they like depending on their line of specialisation, experience and popularity. They usually work according to either:

- a percentage of the total cost (this can amount to between 10 and 15%); or
- an hourly rate

Using an architect in the early planning stages of an extension can avoid later design problems. You may be able to reduce costs by:

- obtaining preliminary sketches of design ideas from your architect and doing your own drawings;
- doing the preliminary drawings and asking your architect to do the final design; or
- supervising the construction yourself and using an architect as a consultant.

DOING IT YOURSELF
Doing it yourself can be very rewarding if you have the time, if you're brave enough and a bit of a risk taker, as you can either hit or miss if you do not have at least some building experience.

Talking to friends who have opted to take the DIY route will fill you with admiration; they will say that the experience was like redesigning the wheel, as the knowledge that builders and architects can take for granted needs to be learned. DIY-ers are motivated by the desire to learn, create and understand their environment, along with the belief that it will save money and bring a sense of achievement and fulfilment.

What do you need to do-it-yourself?

- You need a thorough knowledge of building methods, managerial expertise, and public relations skills to supervise and direct labourers and contractors on site.
- You need to manage your project well or you may find yourself living on a building site which does not seem to have a completion date. Money may run out and the enthusiasm you started with can turn into frustration.
- There is a certain amount of skill required in building homes and extensions, and it is important to have a basic understanding of good building practice before you attempt to do-it-yourself.
- You need to be aware of the particular methods of construction that are suitable for your climatic area. For example, in the Cape one builds with cavity walls due to the winter rainfall and driving rain conditions experienced there.
- You need to know the principles of waterproofing your building to prevent damp penetration.

Time

The DIY-er needs time to familiarise him- or herself with the building process, electrical works, and plumbing works. This learning curve can be minimised by using a professional. The DIY-er who wants to design and build an extension needs to allow as much time as possible to create the design and to organise all the construction materials and labour required.

Important considerations

- Ensure that you give yourself enough time to create the design that suits your requirements and your budget.
- Make a list of your needs.
- Assess exactly what you have and consider where the best area is to extend your home.
- Check your local authority regulations regarding building lines and height restrictions.
- Prepare a sketch of what you want and take it to an architect or designer for critical assessment. S/he will tell

you whether your idea is feasible, whether your plan is suitable and advise you on alternatives. S/he will be able to alert you to ideas that may over-extend your budget and suggest the most economical design for achieving your dreams.

- You may need to ask an architect or a draftsman to draw plans for submission to the local authorities for approval, if you do not want to perform this task yourself.
- While the plans are being approved, you need to consider how you are going to manage the actual building of the extension. Management is critical as you will be working with different materials which you will need to accurately quantify and cost.
- As you will be using both skilled and unskilled labour for the building work, find out about the most suitable standard building contract from the Builders' Institute. Simple matters, such as a fixed cost and time scales for the completion of different elements of the work are often misunderstood.
- Familiarise yourself with building jargon (skirtings, cornices, eaves, etc.) by sourcing a good building dictionary or glossary.
- Find out how subcontractors work – for example, plumbers and electricians – as you will need to employ their expertise. They may have reliable contacts whom you will be able to depend on.

ADVANTAGES OF THE DIY APPROACH
- You can save up to 40% on costs, excluding the cost of your time.
- Doing it yourself gives you a sense of achievement and empowerment.
- It is a significant learning experience.
- You have complete control over the building project and the finishes.

DISADVANTAGES OF THE DIY APPROACH
- It is difficult to set a completion date and you may end up tired of the project and taking short cuts to complete the work.
- You may need to do the work over weekends if you are employed during the week.
- You may end up paying far more than you expected. There are always unanticipated costs due to your lack of building experience.
- It may be impossible to get poor workmanship re-done without the professional status to back you up if you attempt to manage people who are semi-skilled.
- You will lack the experience to consider options which may be more cost-effective.
- If you require a mortgage bond to finance your building project, this may be difficult to obtain if you are not using professionals.

THE LEGAL SIDE

The legal side is often the neglected aspect of planning a home extension. The plans and specifications for your extension are considered legal documents along with any written agreements with the various people – both professional and technical – who will transform the plans into a reality. There are also local authority regulations that need to be adhered to. They relate to what you can or cannot do and how to set about obtaining plan approval, and whether approval for your extension is required.

BEFORE YOU START

In whose name is the property registered?
Before you can start making any changes to your home, the property needs to be registered in your name or legally owned by you. When you buy a property and need to alter or extend it before you move in, legal transfer has to have occurred and the property needs to be registered in your name. The time factor linked to this requirement is often not considered when buying a home that you intend extending. There are some local authorities that will accept written permission from the previous owner (with an attached Power of Attorney) to start building before transfer has taken place.

PROPERTY TITLE DEEDS

What are property title deeds?
This is a document containing or constituting evidence of ownership of a property, registered and sealed at the deeds office. There are usually conditions relating to the sale of the property and a full set of title deeds should be checked by a competent legal person for any restricting clauses which may affect your planned extension.

Why do you need these?
You need to check the title deeds to ensure that the proposed extension is legal. When plans are submitted to the local authorities for approval, they often call for submission of the title deeds.

Where can I obtain title deeds?
Copies of this document are usually given to you when you purchase a property. Copies can be obtained from the deeds office. You will find the telephone number and address of your local deeds office listed in the telephone directory under Government Departments. The information department of every deeds office will be able to help you to locate copies of your property's title deeds going back to the original land grants.

What restrictions could there be in the title deeds?
- Restrictions most often encountered when planning an extension relate to building lines. You are usually prohibited from building over the building lines of your

property as specified in the title deeds and this is usually confirmed by the local town planning regulations. Garages to be built on the front boundary are usually affected by these regulations.

- Restrictions related to the use of your home – for example, forbidding its use for business – may also affect your proposal if you wish to build an extension to work from home.
- There are usually restrictions related to the number of dwellings allowed on a particular property. There may be a restriction on the number of kitchen spaces you can have and, in turn, this may limit your ideas about adding a granny flat to your property or changing your home into a guest house.

How do I deal with restrictions if I find them?

The removal of restrictions from title deeds to meet your requirements is a complicated, costly and time-consuming process, involving your local authority and legal professionals. You can expect to pay around R2 000 for this and to wait up to a year before the restrictive clauses are removed if there are no objections from neighbours. This route is only recommended as a last resort.

LOCAL AUTHORITY APPROVAL

When do I need approval for a planned extension?

You will need local authority approval whenever you plan to make any building changes to your home.

If the changes are minor, such as moving doors, windows or internal walls, you can submit your plans as a 'minor works application' which is less costly and takes less time to approve than a full plan submission.

However, most planned extensions need to be presented to the local authority as a full submission with drawings and a submission and scrutiny fee will be due.

Why do I need approval by the local authorities?

It is illegal to build on your property without local authority approval. Once the plans have been approved, the local authority requires commencement and completion documentation. They will send building inspectors to approve foundation trenches and plumbing pipes before they are covered by earth.

Where can I find out about regulations?

Your architect will be able to advise you on these, but if you are not using an architect it is best to approach the building plans examiner at your local authority's building survey department.

TOWN PLANNING/ZONING REGULATIONS

These are specific to each city or town and are usually specified in the town planning/zoning scheme document compiled by the town planning department and implemented by the zoning department of your local authority. Copies of these documents can be obtained from your local authority but will need to be explained in detail so that you can determine what is relevant to your extension. The regulations cover:

- building lines and setbacks;
- height and number of storeys permitted; and
- site coverage.

Your local authority zoning department will be able to advise you on this information and the town planning department (not often approached for home extensions) will deal with specific concerns such as road widening or rezoning.

BUILDING REGULATIONS

The National Building Regulations (SABS 0400) document, which can be obtained from the South African Bureau of Standards covers all regulations related to building works including: minimum room sizes, ceiling heights, ventilation, natural light, requirements for disabled people, structural considerations, roof materials and pitch, walls, and safety and fire regulations.

Your local authority plans examiner will be able to advise you on the regulations that will apply specifically to your home extension.

The SABS 0400 document is divided into actual regulations and 'deemed to satisfy' rules. The actual regulations are not restrictive and leave room for interpretation by your professional advisers (architects and engineers), whereas the 'deemed to satisfy' rules are more specific, suggesting ways to abide by the regulations. These rules are not enforceable.

These regulations are applied on a national basis. You will also need to ensure that your proposed extension conforms to the town planning/zoning regulations which are specific to each city.

OTHER LOCAL AUTHORITY DEPARTMENTS YOU MAY NEED TO CONSULT

- *Drainage and sewerage:* for the addition of any sewer or rainwater connections from your property to the municipal sewers and stormwater pipes.
- *Roads:* for the implementation of new pavement crossings accessing your property from the street.
- *Survey:* to confirm your site dimensions. A site diagram with the north point, site dimensions, names of surrounding streets and distances to nearest cross-streets needs to be included with the plans that are submitted to the local authority.
- *Structural engineers:* to check that the structural details are sound and that the relevant elements of your extension have been designed by a structural engineer. You may need to submit a structural engineer's certificate with your plans, confirming that specific structural aspects have been designed and will be supervised by a registered structural engineer.

WHAT IF THE PROPOSED EXTENSION DOES NOT COMPLY WITH REGULATIONS?

You will need to apply for a departure from the regulations or apply to the authorities for consent to do what you require. You may need the consent of neighbours and the local authority's approval for some departures (sometimes called 'waivers').

The procedure and fees for obtaining these departures can be confirmed by your building plans examiner.

WHAT HAPPENS IF PLANS ARE NOT SUBMITTED?

Proceeding with building work without approval is a criminal offence. You can be taken to court by the local authority, instructed to demolish the extensions, or asked to submit plans for approval of 'as-built work'.

AGREEMENTS WITH PROFESSIONAL CONSULTANTS

Confirm in writing the appointment of any consultants (architects, designers, structural engineers) if they do not issue you with a standard letter of appointment. This written agreement should cover:

- what they will do for you;
- their fees and when they become due; and
- how long it will take to complete the work.

It is vital to be informed about these aspects of your relationship with your professionals as they are acting as your agents and on your behalf. It is important that you understand exactly what they will do for you and what it will cost. Knowing these factors up front will prevent surprises later and will help to maintain a good relationship with your consultants.

Consulting fees need to be included in the overall budget for your home extension. If properly used and competent, these professionals should be able to save you money and offer good advice.

BUILDERS AND STANDARD BUILDING CONTRACTS

It is compulsory for builders and contractors to be registered with the Industrial Council. If they wish, they can become members of the Master Builders' Association (MBA) and the Building Industries' Federation of South Africa (BIFSA), the official mouthpiece of organised building and allied industries, which regulates business and trade relations with unions, public and professional bodies. The federation protects the interests of members and arranges recruitment, education and training.

Not all builders and contractors are members, and it is prudent to ask your builder for proof of registration and membership of these professional bodies. This is important if you want to have some form of recourse about bad workmanship, especially if you are working without consulting an architect.

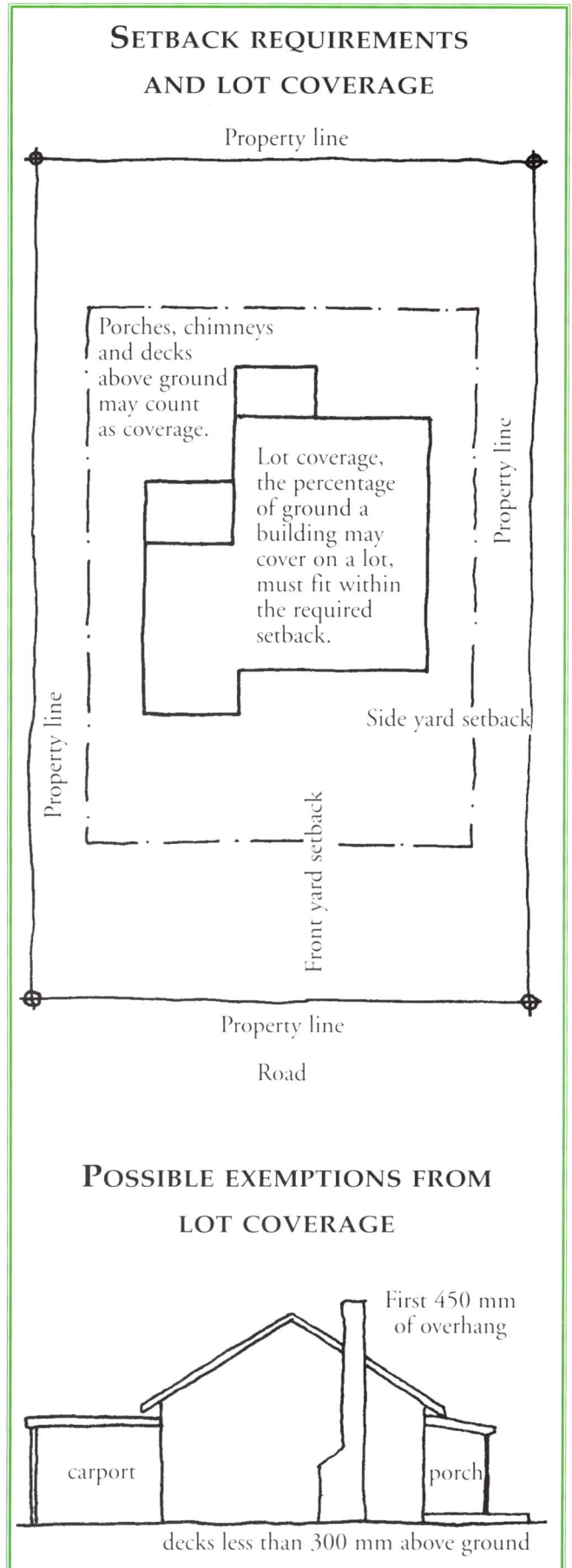

SETBACK REQUIREMENTS AND LOT COVERAGE

Property line

Porches, chimneys and decks above ground may count as coverage.

Lot coverage, the percentage of ground a building may cover on a lot, must fit within the required setback.

Property line

Property line

Side yard setback

Front yard setback

Property line

Road

POSSIBLE EXEMPTIONS FROM LOT COVERAGE

First 450 mm of overhang

carport

porch

decks less than 300 mm above ground

MOVE OUT OR LIVE IN WHILE BUILDING?

There are pros and cons to living in your home during the building of your extension.

LIVING IN

PROS
• Control over building work and supervision.
• Being able to pick up problems quickly.
• Night-time security.

CONS
• Dust, noise, builders' materials, scaffolding and rubble on your property.
• Workmen on site during the day.
• Times when your water and electricity need to be temporarily cut off.
• Times when you are without a kitchen and/or a bathroom.

MOVING OUT

PROS
• Being away from the noise, dust and workmen.
• The builder is able to work quickly and effectively without worrying about disturbances.
• Less stress as you are not completely immersed in the building process.
• Temporary cutting off of services such as telephone and electricity will not affect you.

CONS
• Less control over what is happening on site.
• Less security on site (although the builder assumes this responsibility when you have moved out).

THINGS TO AVOID

To ensure that your home extension project runs smoothly and that you survive what can be a very stressful process, here are a few pointers on what to avoid:

Unclear communication
Ensure that from the start that you and your professional and building teams communicate clearly and preferably in writing. Verbal communication can often be misunderstood or forgotten. If you ever need to prove that you issued instructions to your builder or architect, this may be difficult if they have not been recorded. If you employ an architect, never give direct instructions to the builder or his staff. Working only through the architect will prevent potential mismanagement.

Changes once building has started on site
Although changes are sometimes inevitable, they always prove costly. Once your builder is on site, he will follow his own schedule to complete work on time and co-ordinate his tradesmen (plumbers, electricians, etc.) to do the work in the most economical way.

If you alter your requirements, it often causes delay and will more than likely add costs to the original quote. Also, to record your changes, the architect or designer may need to change the drawings and for this there will also be a fee. Having mentioned this, however, it is not always easy to read and understand drawings and we encourage you to ask your architect, designer or draftsman to explain any aspects of the drawings which are not clear to you on presentation. The financial effect of changes to the drawings is not always considered and it is important to ask your builder and architect to advise you on costs before the changes are effected.

Misunderstanding documents and drawings

Ensure that you fully understand the drawings and documents that you sign. Ask your architect to explain any items on the drawings and any clauses in the standard building contracts that you do not understand.

Choosing an architect or builder whom you don't trust

Before you choose your builder, ask for references and check the work that s/he has done previously. Speak to the owners of completed extensions and ask them what s/he was like to work with. Remember, your architect does not choose your builder for you (although s/he may, in good faith, recommend builders) and it is your responsibility to make sure that you are satisfied with the quality of work that your builder is capable of before appointing him/her. Similarly, check the record of your architect or any other consultant whom you employ to ensure that you get a recommended service. Once you have appointed your professional team, you need to trust that they are all working in your best interests. There is nothing more off-putting to a builder, architect or builder's team than having an owner who is suspicious or feels that s/he is in some way being cheated.

Vagueness regarding the roles of your team

Be aware of whom you employ and your agreed relationship. Ensure you are clear about the architect's and the builder's roles and what they are contracted to do.

Do not give instructions on site (when you employ an architect and builder)

Giving instructions to workmen on site who are employed by your builder removes the authority of your builder and architect and can lead to costly mistakes. If you employ an architect ensure that all instructions are given through him/her only. If you suspect poor workmanship on site, report it immediately to your architect. Do not stop work on site.

Financial surprises

It is wise to keep about 10 to 15% of your overall building costs available for errors. There are inevitably unanticipated costs, such as having to repair an existing underground pipe which may lie under your proposed extension, or damage to existing property during building work (not caused by the builder). This sum of money is often referred to as a 'contingency amount'.

Jumping to conclusions

Remember that building is a process and that most errors can be satisfactorily corrected. When your building is practically complete and before you move in, it is wise to perform an inspection with the assistance of your architect. Prepare a list of work you are unhappy with and give the builder a set time to attend to repairs before you make a final payment.

HOW TO READ A PLAN OR DRAWING

PLAN

In basic terms, a plan is a diagram of a building drawn as if the entire building has been cut through on the horizontal, about one metre above the ground. Plans are drawn to a scale which can be indicated as a ratio or as a line divided into regular intervals. For example 1:100 means that every 1 mm on the drawing represents 100 mm in reality. Therefore, a measurement of 10 mm on a drawing represents 1 000 mm or 1 m in reality. You can measure directly off a plan, without having to calculate the conversion, using a scale ruler. The examples in this book use a one-metre measurement guide.

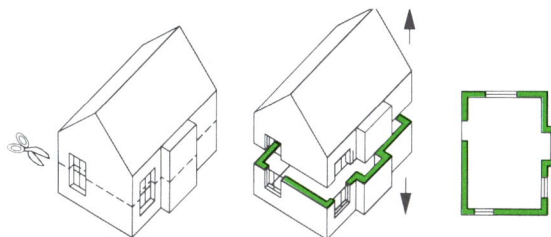

SECTION

A section is a vertical 'cut' through a building. The position and direction of the cut are indicated on the plan. The aspects which lie beyond the line of the cut are usually shown as an elevation.

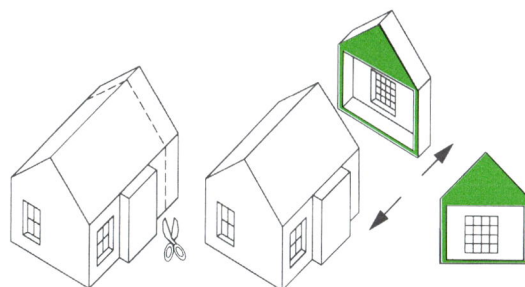

ELEVATION

Elevations are drawings of the sides of the building which are drawn as if you were looking at the side square-on. Each elevation is named according to the direction from which it is being viewed. For example, the north elevation is the elevation seen if you stand to the north of the building.

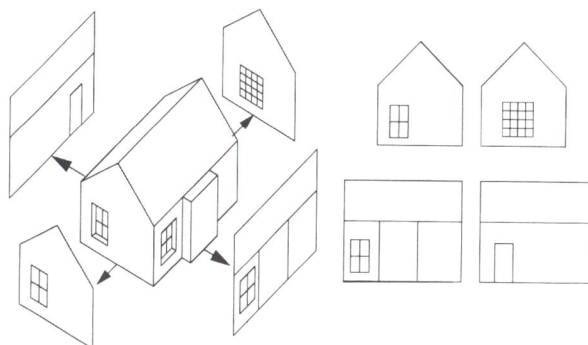

SYMBOLS USED ON THE PLAN

Existing walls	Spiral stair
New walls	Counter tops or cupboards
Demolished walls	Sliding door
Paving	Roof windows
Double doors	New extension
Single door	Double bed
Window	Single bed
WC	Table and chairs
Bath	3 seater couch
Shower	2 seater couch
Washbasin	Seat
Sink	Vanity basin
Stair	Oven

REMODELLING EXISTING SPACE

It is not always necessary to add space to create new rooms. You can rearrange or remodel existing space by moving the position of bathrooms and kitchens, removing or adding internal walls, and adding doors and windows.

- Removing an existing wall can transform two small rooms into a single large space.
- Removing walls can turn wasted space into a usable room.
- You may not like the way the house flows to the garden. Installing double doors to a patio and creating a living space close to the garden may be a solution.
- You can change an existing entrance hall into a large living space.
- You can relocate bathrooms and add an en-suite to the main bedroom.
- You can convert a room into a guest suite with its own entrance.

- A new wall can create a passage from the living area to the bedrooms, or create private space within a larger room.
- Add half walls, windows in the walls or remove a portion of a wall if you do not want the space to be completely separate. This allows for flow over or through the walls.
- You can find a way to view your back garden from the front door and bring light to dark passages.
- You can create openings in walls to special views. This will also add light and ventilation to a space.
- Wherever possible try to position a window on two walls in each room to get an even spread of sunlight and prevent glare from having only one opening.

This home is extended at the back and a new timber deck leads to the garden where a river runs through the property. The back section of the roof is extended to cover the new room arrangement. A triangular gable window has been added to the new back living area so that as you walk through the front door one can see a mountain view. The feeling of space is created by the flow of light through the extension and by allowing the ceilings of the new extension to follow the roof shape. What started off as a small home with passages and small rooms has been converted into a home with a large open-plan living space leading to a timber deck which overlooks the previously inaccessible river garden.

The original kitchen and bathroom were removed as they were located exactly where one would want a living area. The original kitchen led out to a shaded back courtyard which, in turn, led to the river garden. The bathroom window also faced the river garden, but the view of this asset was obscured.

The kitchen and bathrooms were relocated at the sides of the house. The kitchen was located on the driveway side and a carport was added to give covered access from the driveway to the kitchen.

A room on the opposite side of the house, near the bedrooms, was converted into two bathrooms – one for general and guest use, and the other en-suite from the main bedroom. The main bedroom now has its own set of glazed doors to the new timber deck.

The original garage and store were converted into staff/guest quarters with a separate entrance. This facility has a room and a bathroom and also leads to the terraced river garden.

Before plan

1. Bedroom
2. Bedroom
3. Living room
4. Dining room
5. Kitchen
6. Stoep
7. Garage
8. Store

0m 1m 2m 3m 4m 5m

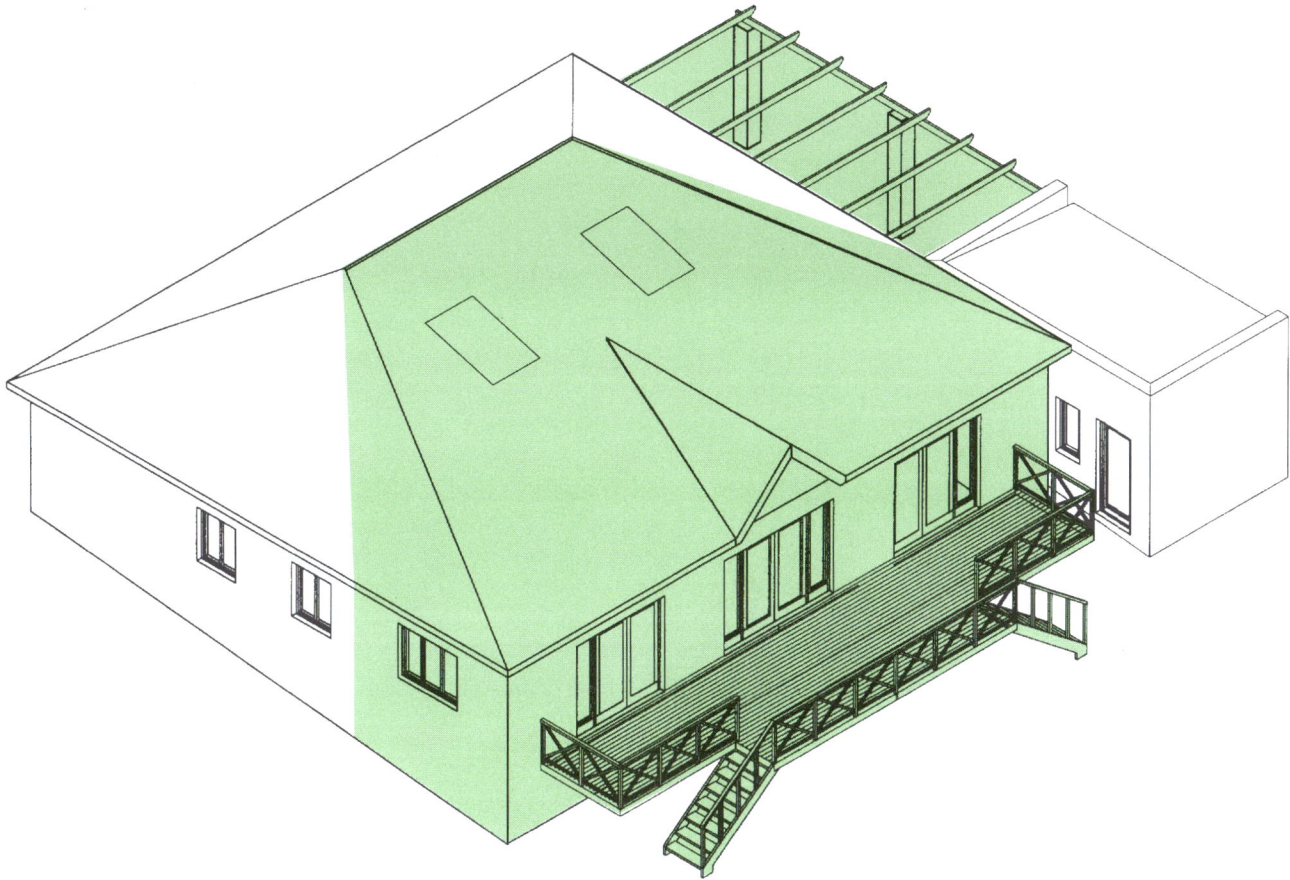

After plan

1. Bedroom
2a. Bathroom
2b. Bathroom
3. Bedroom
4. Kitchen
5. Dining room, with roof windows
6. Living room
7a. Staff/guest quarters
7b. Bathroom
8. Store
9. Bedroom
10. Timber deck
11. Carport

This plan shows the addition of a bay window downstairs, a deck upstairs, a garage extension and remodelled space. The existing kitchen and dining room were incorporated into one large kitchen/dining living space with new French doors leading to a new swimming pool patio. A new bay window was also added. The original house had no flow from the inside to the swimming pool area.

Upstairs, an enclosed balcony was incorporated in a small bedroom to create a large main bedroom. An existing passage and part of the original enclosed balcony were converted into the en-suite bathroom for the new bedroom and a timber deck was added which leads off this room through French doors. From the new timber deck, there is a magnificent mountain view and a private place to sit away from the rest of the family who mostly use the new kitchen space off the swimming pool patio. The timber deck has the added bonus of creating a covered area for the existing side patio.

An existing upstairs bathroom was demolished and the space is now used as a separate study. The single garage was extended to become a secure double garage leading to a kitchen yard which allows undercover access from the garage to the house.

The ease of flow from the interior to the garden has improved significantly.

Before ground-floor plan

1. Single garage
2. Bedroom
3. Bathroom
4. Living room
5. Dining room
6. Store
7. Kitchen
8. Drying yard
9. Staff bedroom and WC
10. Patio

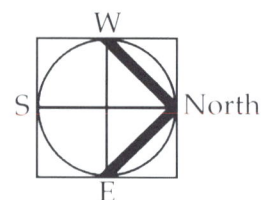

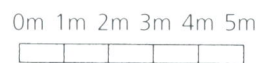

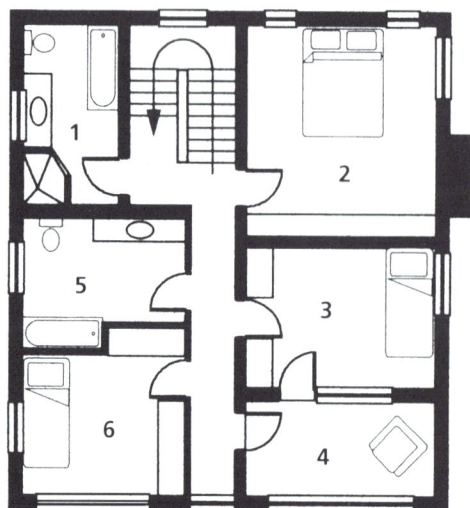

0m 1m 2m 3m 4m 5m

Before upper-floor plan

1. Bathroom
2. Main bedroom
3. Bedroom
4. Enclosed balcony
5. Bathroom
6. Bedroom

After ground-floor plan

1. Double garage,
   with door to yard
2. Guest bedroom
3. Bathroom
4. Formal lounge/dining area
5. Open-plan living space,
   with new bay window
   and doors to patio
6. Laundry
7. Open-plan kitchen
8. Drying yard
9. Staff bedroom and WC
10. Deck
11. Patio
12. Swimming pool

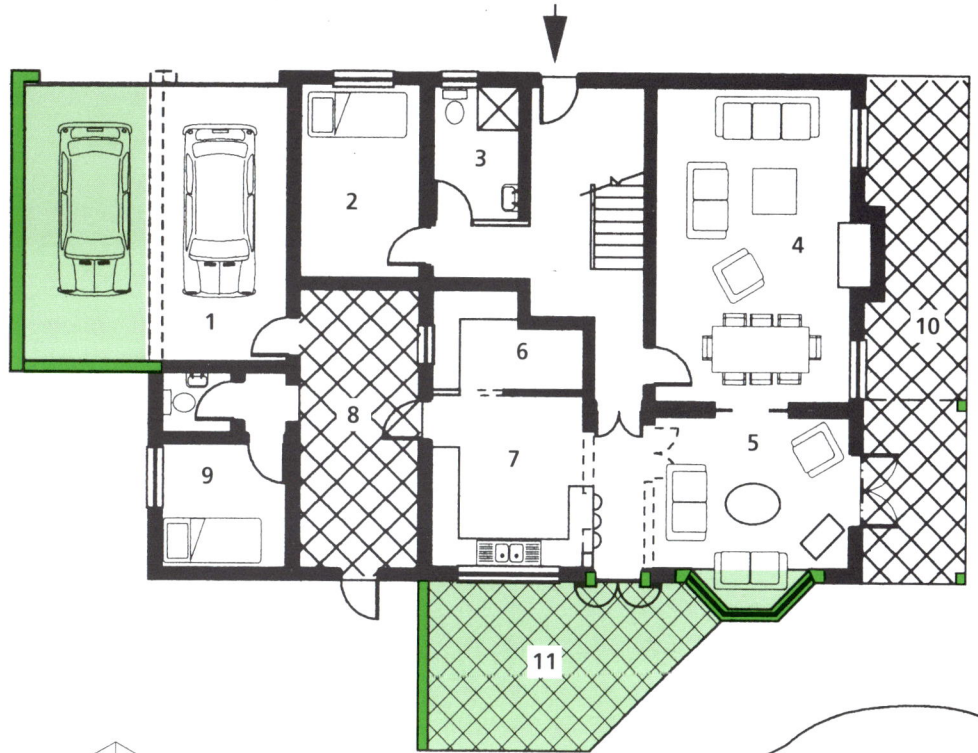

After upper-floor plan

1. Study
2. Bedroom
3. Bedroom, with doors to deck
4. En-suite bathroom
5. Bathroom
6. Bedroom
7. Timber deck

In this home, an entrance hall was added, the interior was rearranged and an outdoor room was added to the garden side of the house. The existing garage was incorporated into the house and a new covered carport built with secure access from the street. A new street boundary wall with pedestrian gate replaced a dilapidated hedge.

The rooms were rearranged internally so that the converted garage and store became the new main bedroom and en-suite bathroom with its own private courtyard. The new entrance hall opens directly onto a living room which leads into a dining room and through French doors to the new outdoor covered patio. The patio,

in turn, leads off the redesigned kitchen and dining room spaces and these two spaces can be opened up to create a large indoor/outdoor entertaining space if required.

The original staff quarters were converted into a guest suite, and a bay window was added to the small bedroom which has its own private garden.

The children's bedrooms are located on the other side of the living space with a playroom/ study and a door leading to the garden. The original bathroom was converted into a bathroom with a separate guest toilet and shower.

A view through the house from the front door to the back garden has made the home feel larger and filled with light.

0m 1m 2m 3m 4m 5m

Before plan

1. Garage
2. Store
3. Kitchen
4. Living room
5. Bedroom
6. Bathroom
7. Bedroom
8. Lounge
9. Dining room
10. Bathroom
11. Bedroom

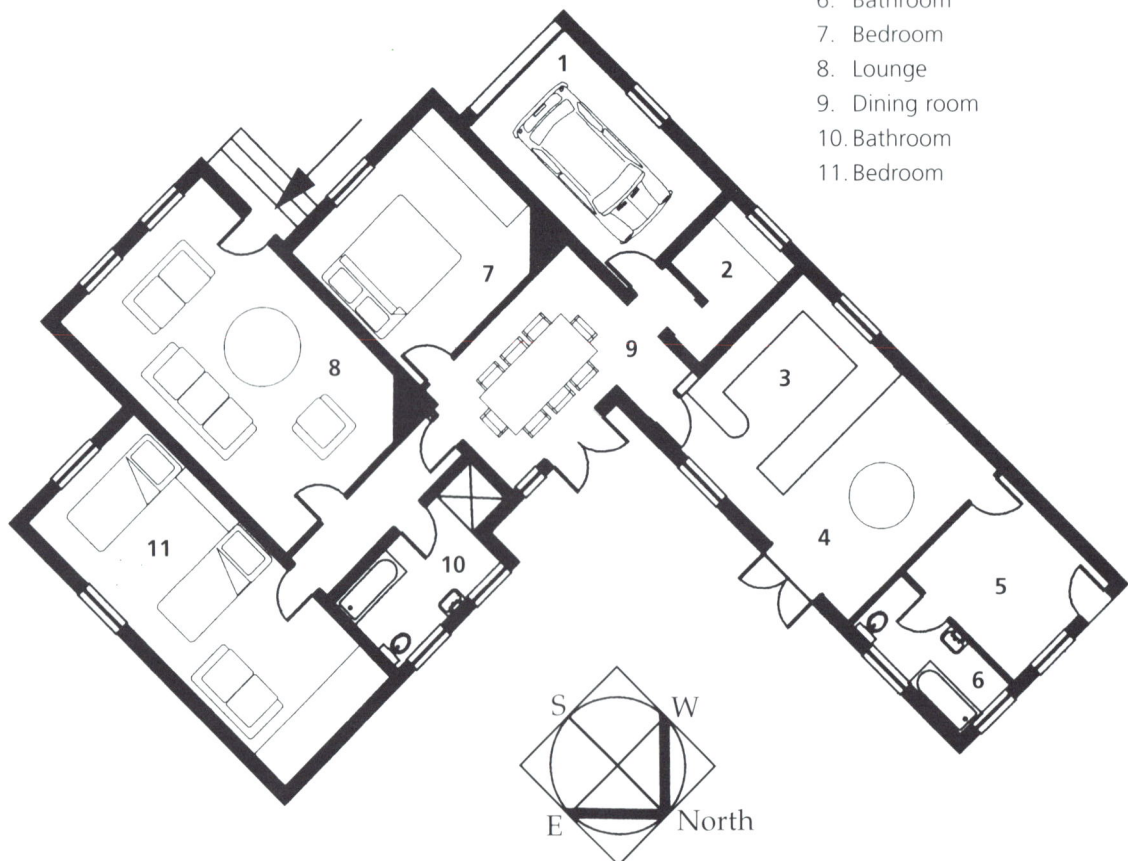

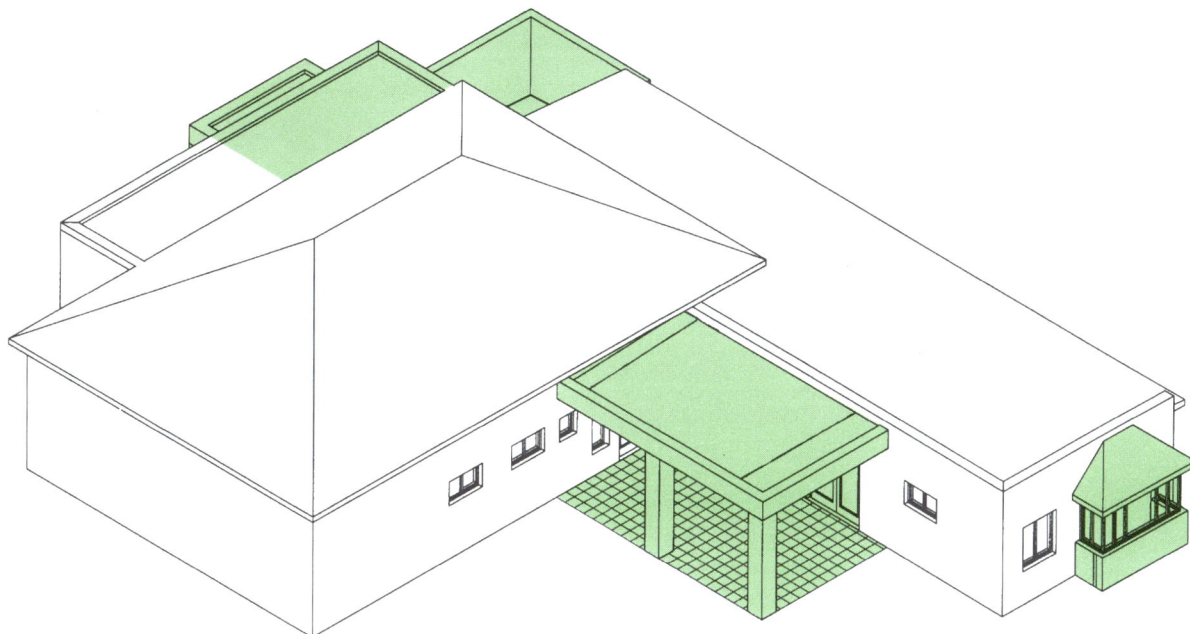

After plan

1. Main bedroom (converted garage), with doors to private courtyard
2. Bathroom
3. Kitchen
4. Playroom
5. Guest bedroom, with new bay window
6. Bathroom
7. Living room
8. Television Room
9. Dining room
10. Bathroom, with shower
11. Bedroom
12. Entrance
13. Private courtyard
14. Covered patio

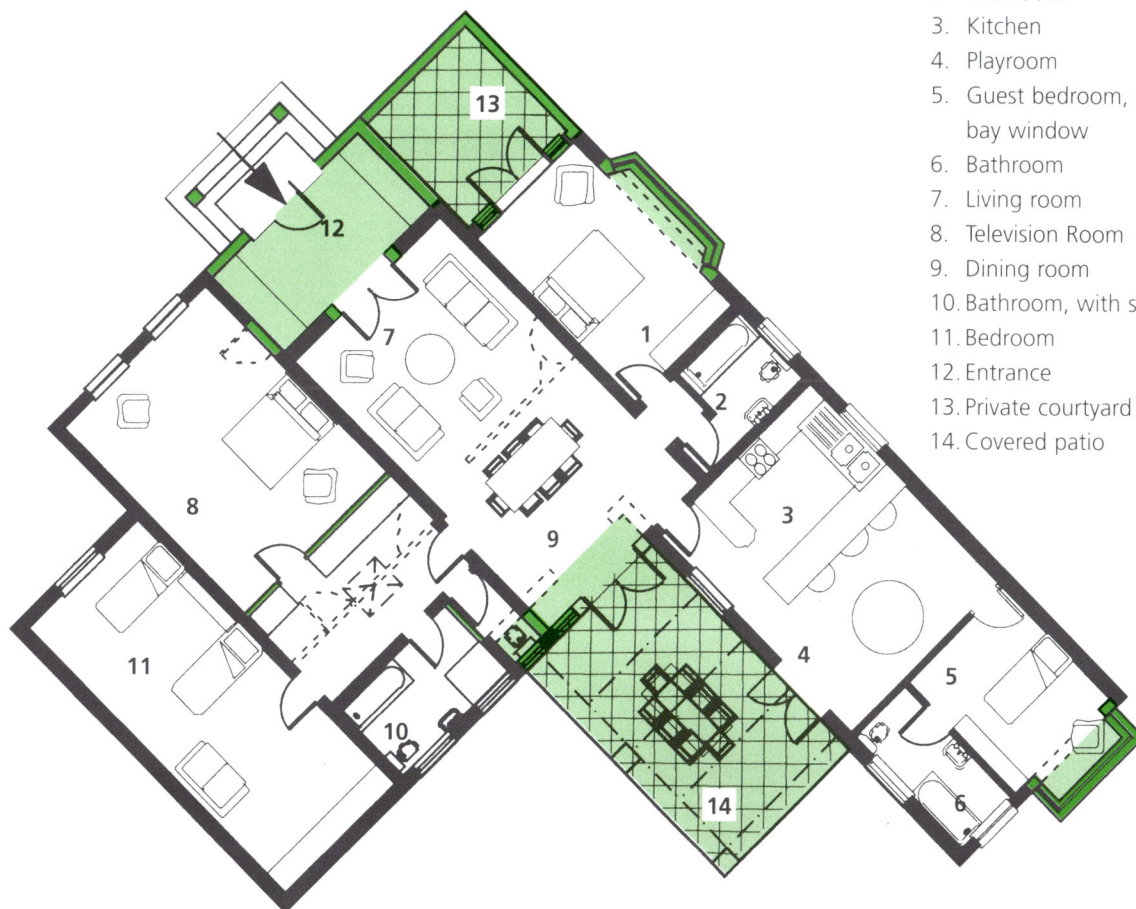

PLAN 4

This large and rambling home, located near the beach, has been converted into three separate units, each with its own entrance, bedrooms, bathrooms and open-plan kitchen/living area. Separate electrical pay meters and telephone lines were also installed in each unit. The owner decided to live in one of the units and rent out the others as fully furnished holiday accommodation.

Two of the units have two bedrooms and two bathrooms and the other central unit has a separate single bedroom and bathroom.

The existing basement garage and store were converted into a four-car garage and a caretaker's flat. There is a stairway from the garage to an upstairs yard space which is covered and leads to each unit. This allows tenants undercover access to their units from the secure garage.

With parking space being at a premium in the area, this facility is an added bonus to the renovated home which is now a financially viable investment for its owners.

In this example, all the existing space was used without any extension to the actual envelope of the building. All changes occurred internally and the external character was maintained. Where possible, existing cupboard and kitchen fittings were reused in the new units to contain the overall conversion costs.

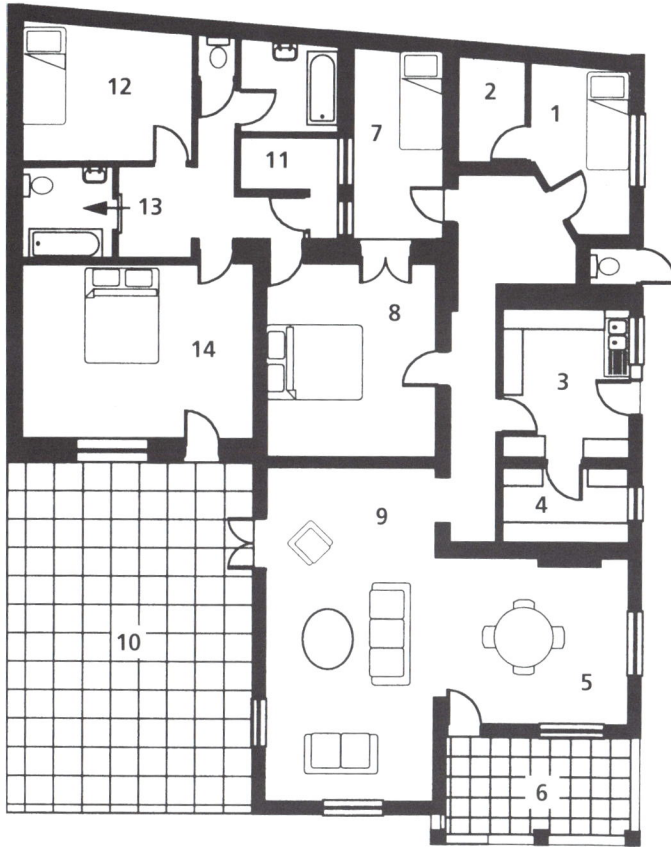

Before plan

1. Bedroom
2. Bathroom
3. Kitchen
4. Store
5. Dining room
6. Entrance porch
7. Bedroom
8. Bedroom
9. Living room
10. Patio
11. Store
12. Bedroom
13. Bathroom
14. Bedroom

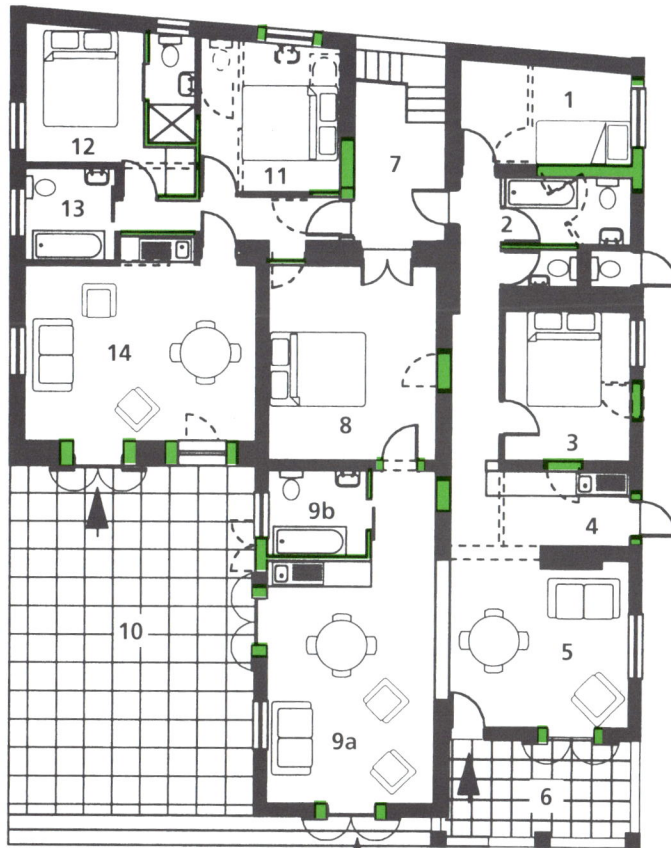

0m 1m 2m 3m 4m 5m

After plan

1. Bedroom
2. Bathroom
3. Bedroom
4. Kitchen
5. Dining/living area
6. Entrance porch
7. Covered yard, with steps to garage
8. Bedroom
9a. Dining/living/kitchen
9b. Bathroom
10. Patio
11. Bedroom (remove bathroom)
12. Bedroom, with en-suite bathroom
13. Bathroom
14. Dining/living/kitchen

UNIT 3   UNIT 2   UNIT 1

29

A garage was made into a living room extension on the north-facing front of the house, and a new garage added at the back.

This house has the advantage of having access roads from two sides and the new garage and staff quarters were relocated on the south side of the house, near to the redesigned kitchen, so that the owners can have secure access from the street to the garage through remote-controlled garage doors and direct undercover access from the garage to the kitchen.

The small kitchen, store and laundry were made into one large live-in kitchen with new French doors to a new back courtyard. An added advantage of this back courtyard is that it gives light to the new kitchen and one can now see through the house from the front to the back. An opening roof light was added to the dining space to bring light and ventilation to this central location.

The front of the house maintained its character and the large front garden is now dedicated to children's play as the original driveway to the garage is no longer necessary.

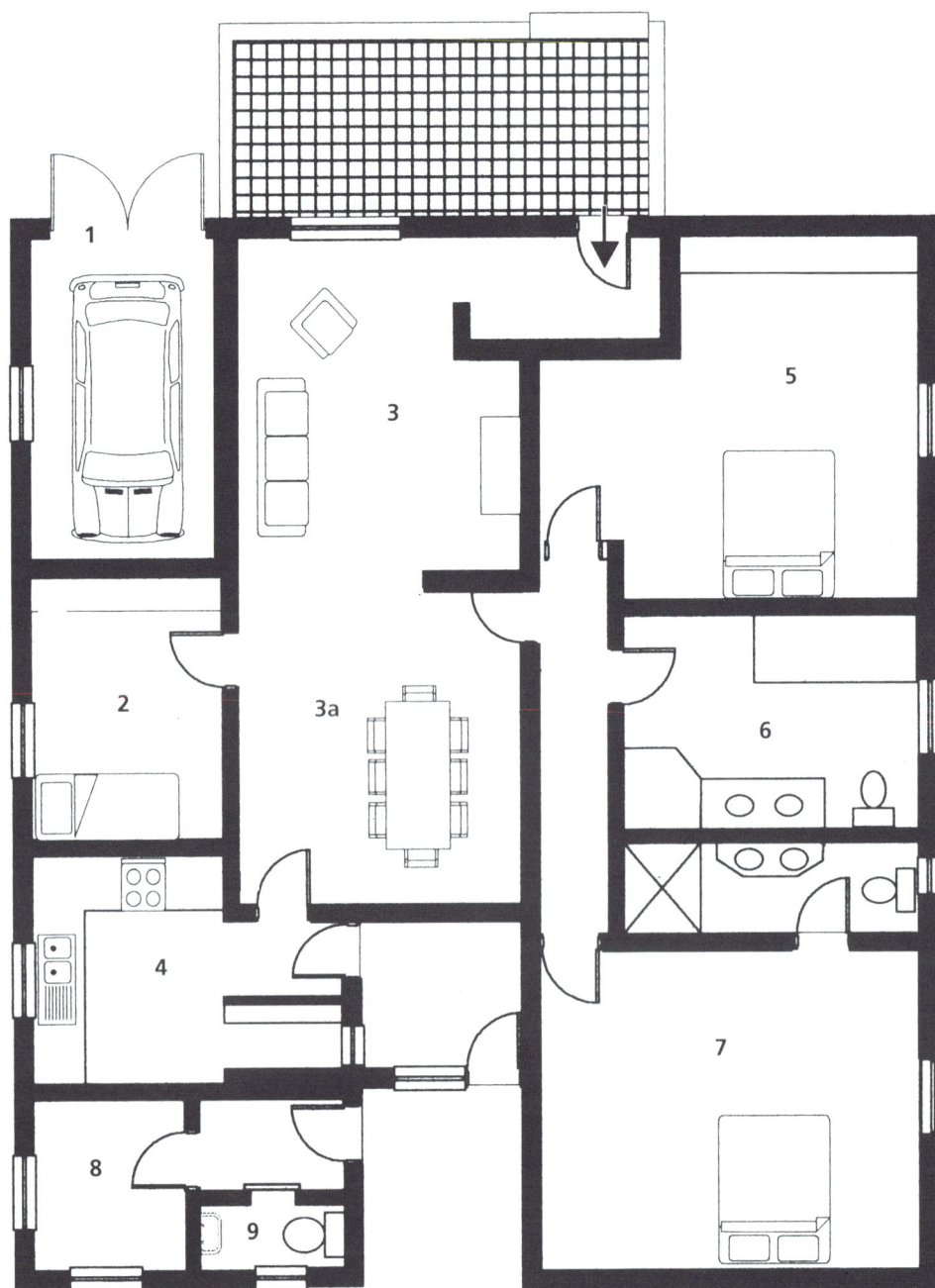

Before plan

1. Garage
2. Bedroom
3. Lounge/dining room
4. Kitchen
5. Bedroom
6. Bathroom
7. Bedroom
8. Store
9. Outside WC

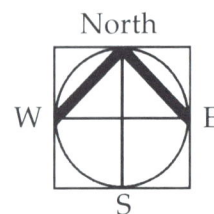

North
W   E
S

After plan

1. Extended lounge
2. Bedroom
3. Dining room
4. Kitchen, with hatch to dining area
5. Bedroom
6. Bathroom
7. Bedroom, with en-suite bathroom
8. Garage
9. Guest bedroom, with en-suite bathroom

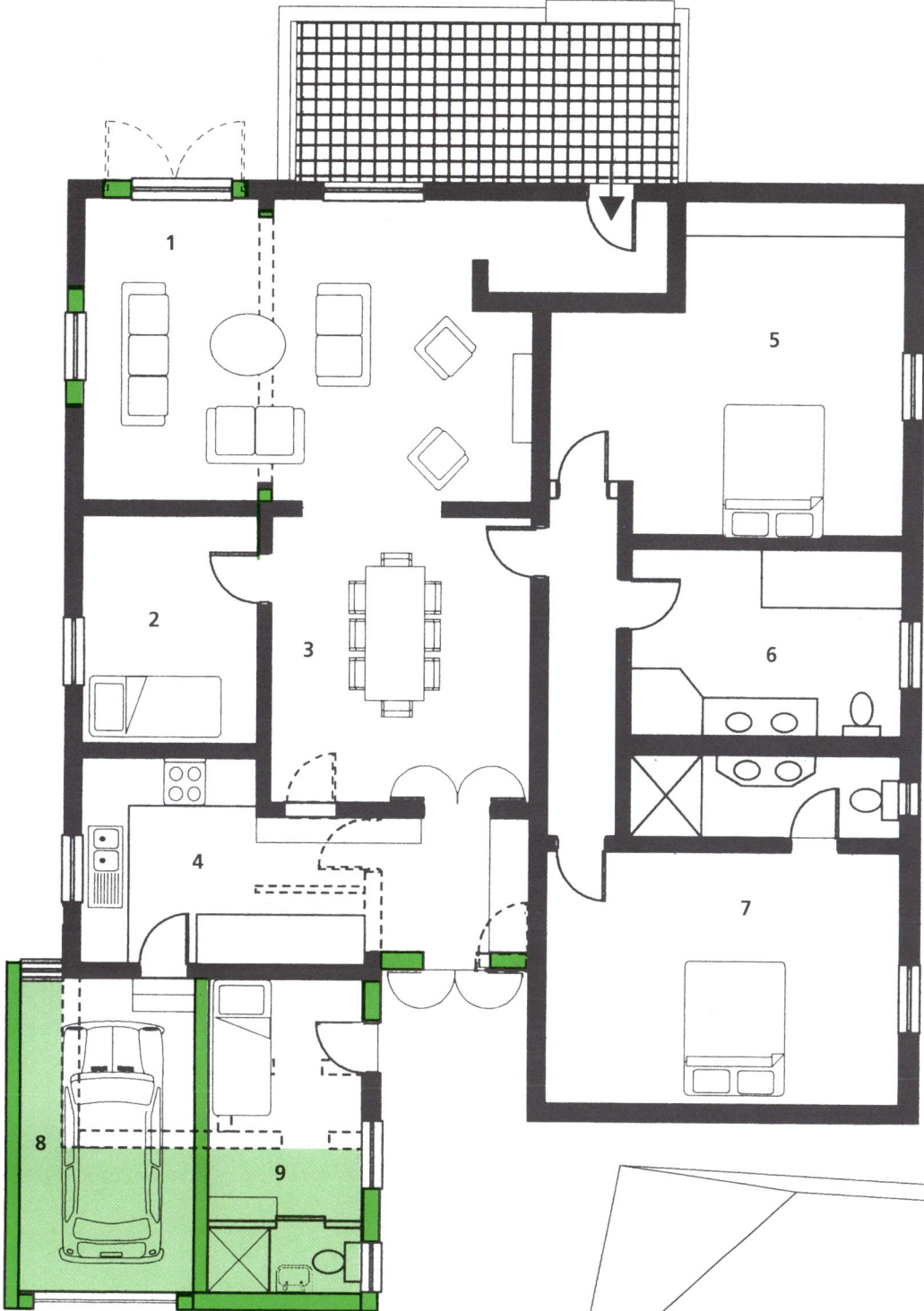

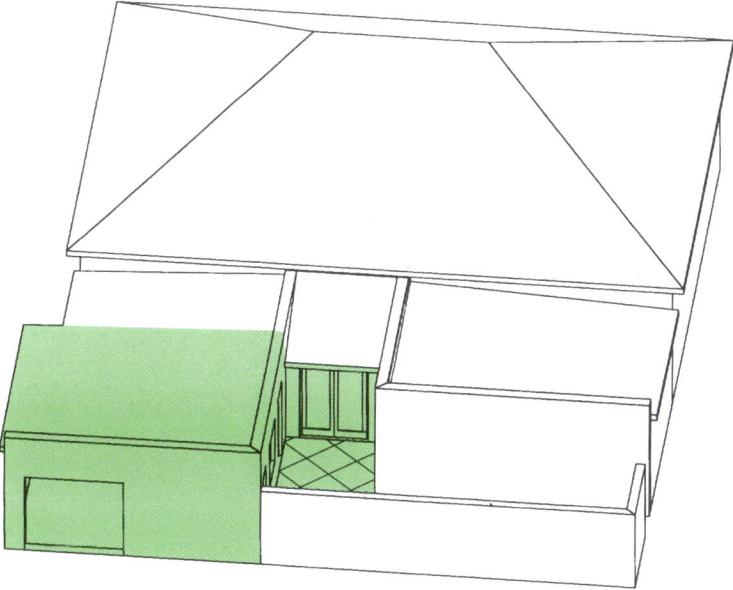

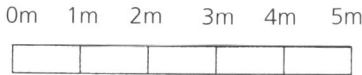

0m 1m 2m 3m 4m 5m

PLAN 6

The existing garage was extended and staff quarters were relocated so that a new large playroom could be gained. This now leads onto a pergola-covered patio off the swimming pool garden.

The new playroom is near to the redesigned kitchen. The flow is good between these spaces and leads directly to the pool garden.

The only extensions to the envelope of this house were the garage and part of the new playroom. Both of these extensions have roofs matching the style of the main house roof: a double-pitched tiled roof with eaves details.

The staff quarters are located off a drying yard leading to the kitchen's back door. The garage has direct undercover access to the main house.

The new patio leads off the new living area and it is finished with a slasto floor and a planted timber pergola. The pergola is supported on facebrick piers to match similar ones around the home and the new balustrade is in keeping with the style of the main house.

The swimming pool garden area now has a usable patio leading off it and the mostly inaccessible side garden can be reached from this new patio and the playroom.

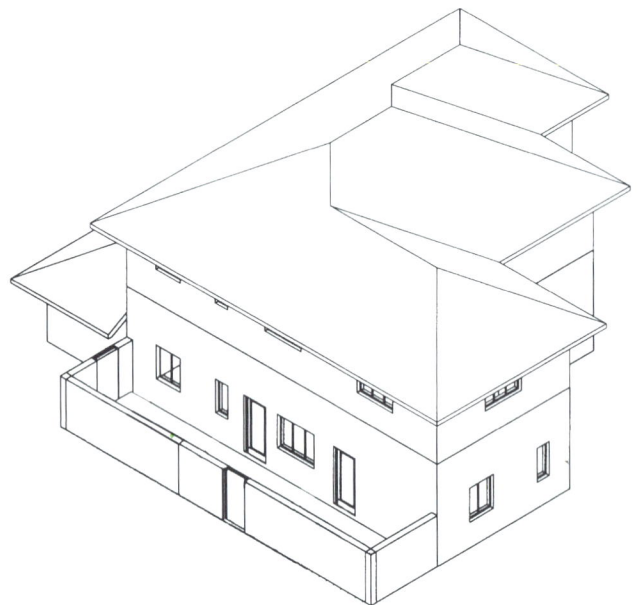

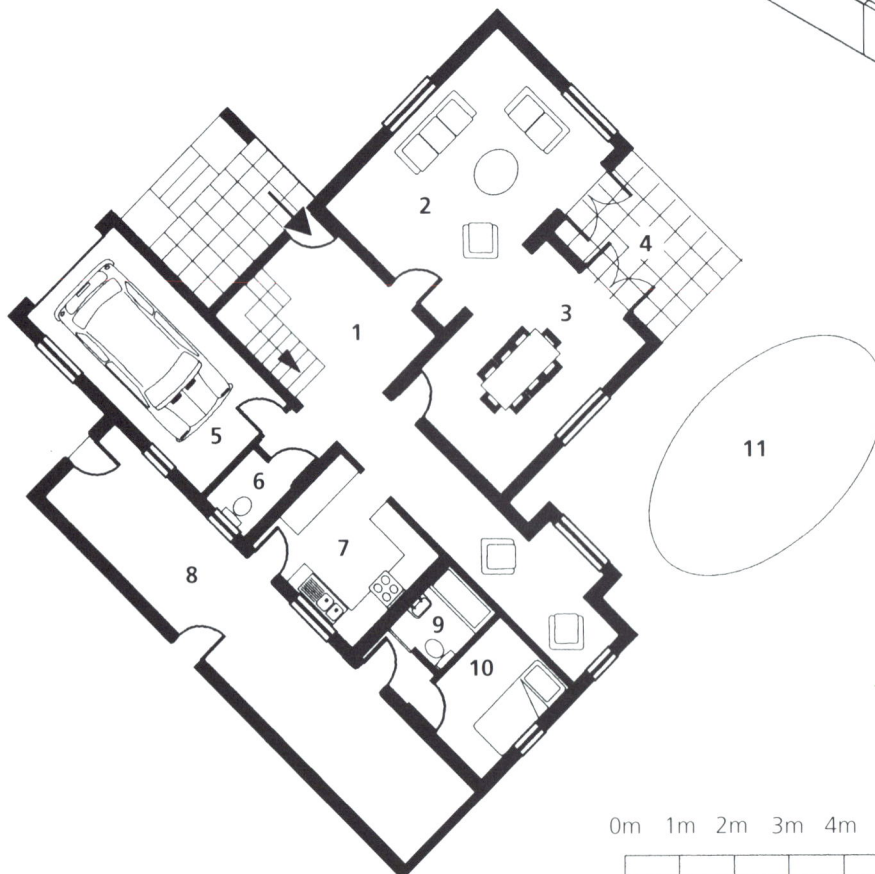

Before plan

1. Entrance hall
2. Living room
3. Dining room
4. Patio
5. Garage
6. WC
7. Kitchen
8. Back yard/patio
9. Bathroom
10. Staff quarters
11. Swimming pool

0m 1m 2m 3m 4m 5m

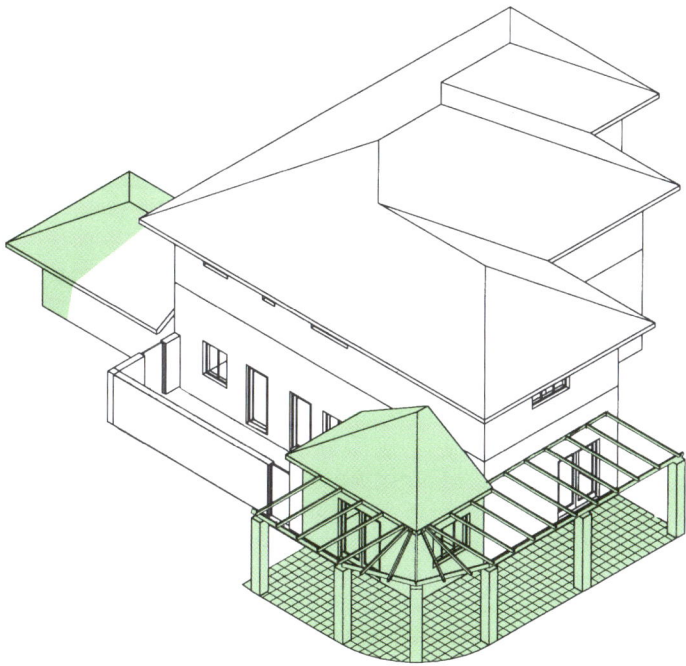

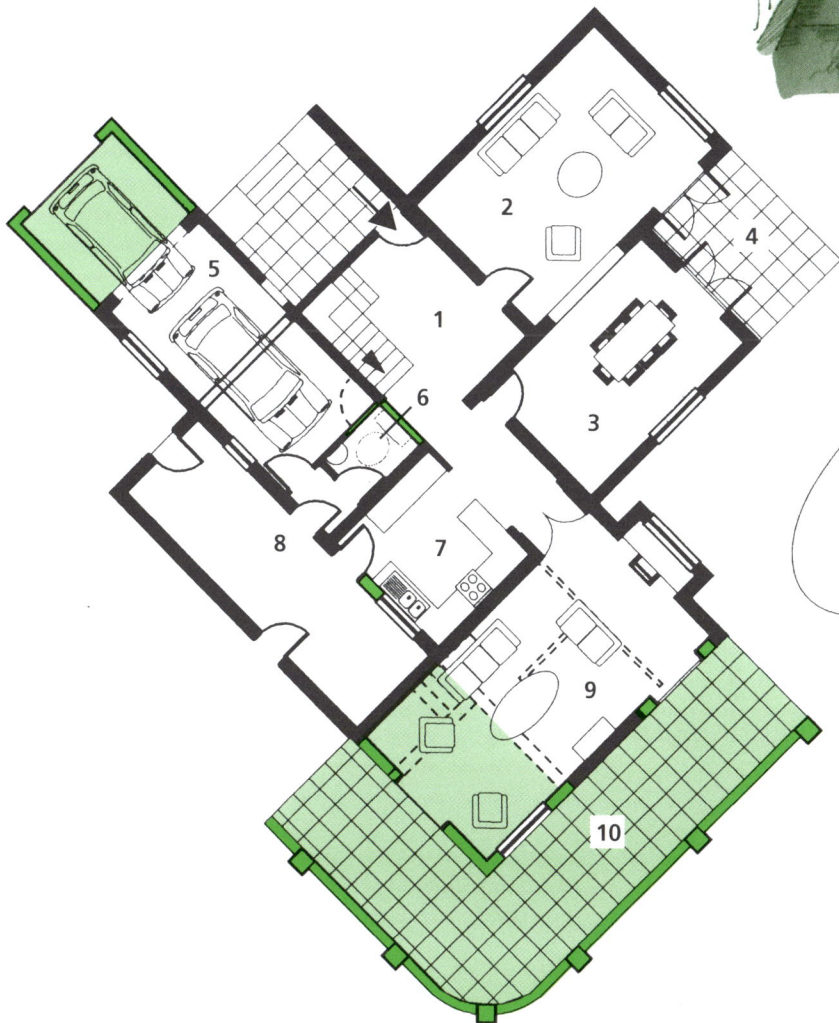

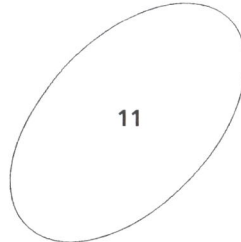

After plan

1. Entrance hall
2. Lounge
3. Dining room
4. Patio
5. Extended garage
6. WC
7. Replanned kitchen
8. Back yard/patio
9. Living room
10. Patio with planted pergola, brick columns and balustrade
11. Swimming pool

A large family needed space for a granny flat so that their grandmother could live with them but have her own private suite with a bedroom, guest room, bathroom, dining room and kitchen.

Downstairs, the existing guest room and bathroom had a door altered and this suite became the new staff quarters which leads off a covered lobby from the kitchen.

The original dilapidated staff quarters located partially under the upper floor was completely renovated and extended to create a large bedroom space, a smaller study/guest room with doors leading out to the north-facing garden, and a new bathroom and kitchen. One of the existing living spaces in the main house was given over to the granny flat for use as a living/dining room.

The original kitchen was divided into two kitchens, each large enough to suit the family's needs.

The grand historic style of this home was maintained with the new extension at the side. It was built in the same style as the main house and many of the teak windows and doors were reused.

The roof tiles used for the main house were also used for the extension. Details of the roof and eaves and the wall finishes – both interior and exterior – match those of the original house.

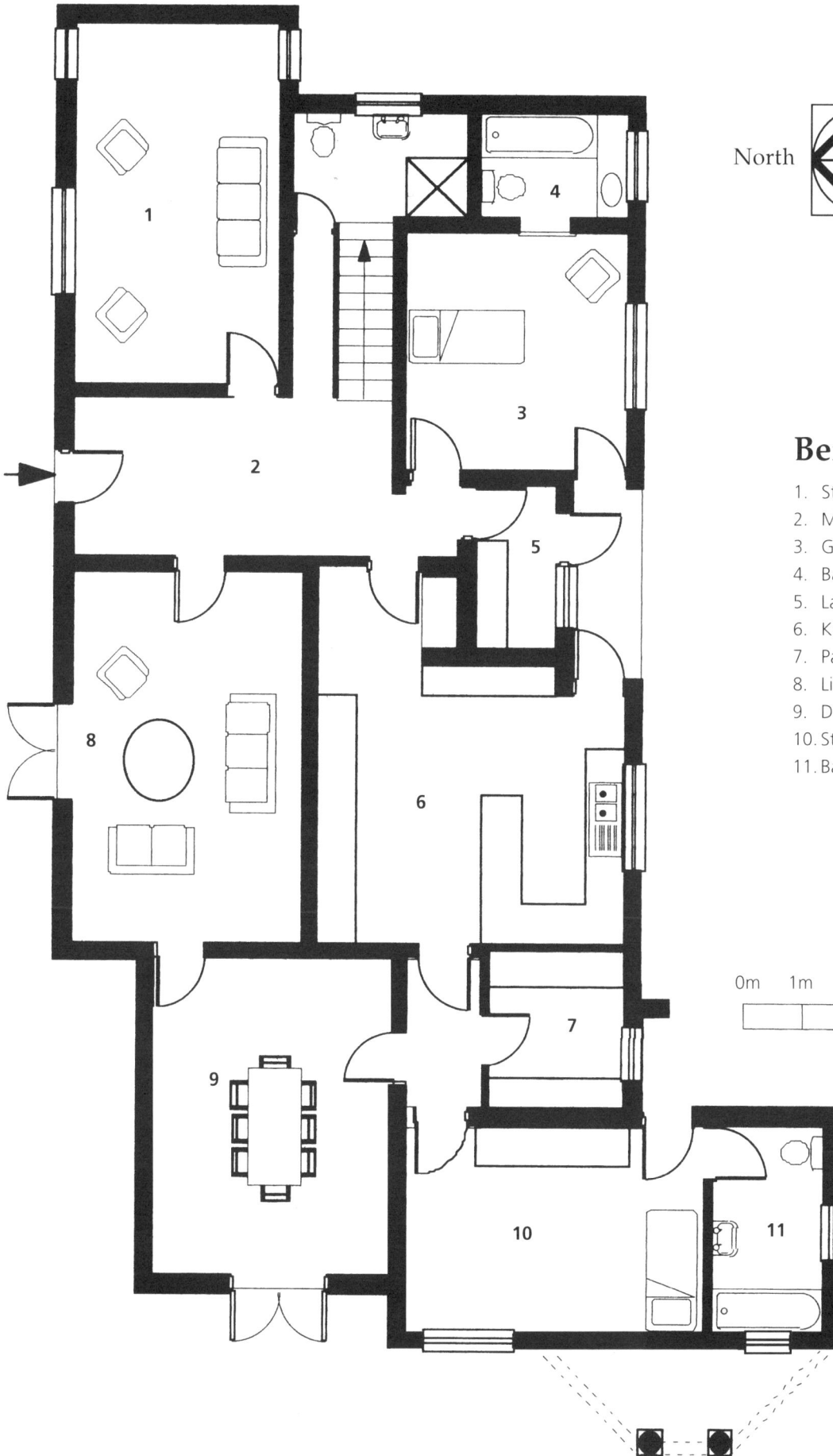

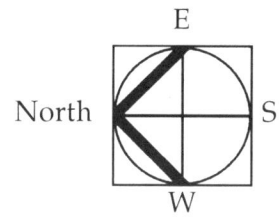

Before plan

1. Study
2. Main entrance hall
3. Guest bedroom
4. Bathroom
5. Laundry
6. Kitchen
7. Pantry
8. Living area
9. Dining area
10. Staff quarters
11. Bathroom

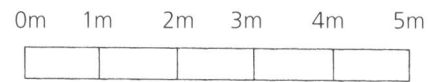

North   E   S   W

0m   1m   2m   3m   4m   5m

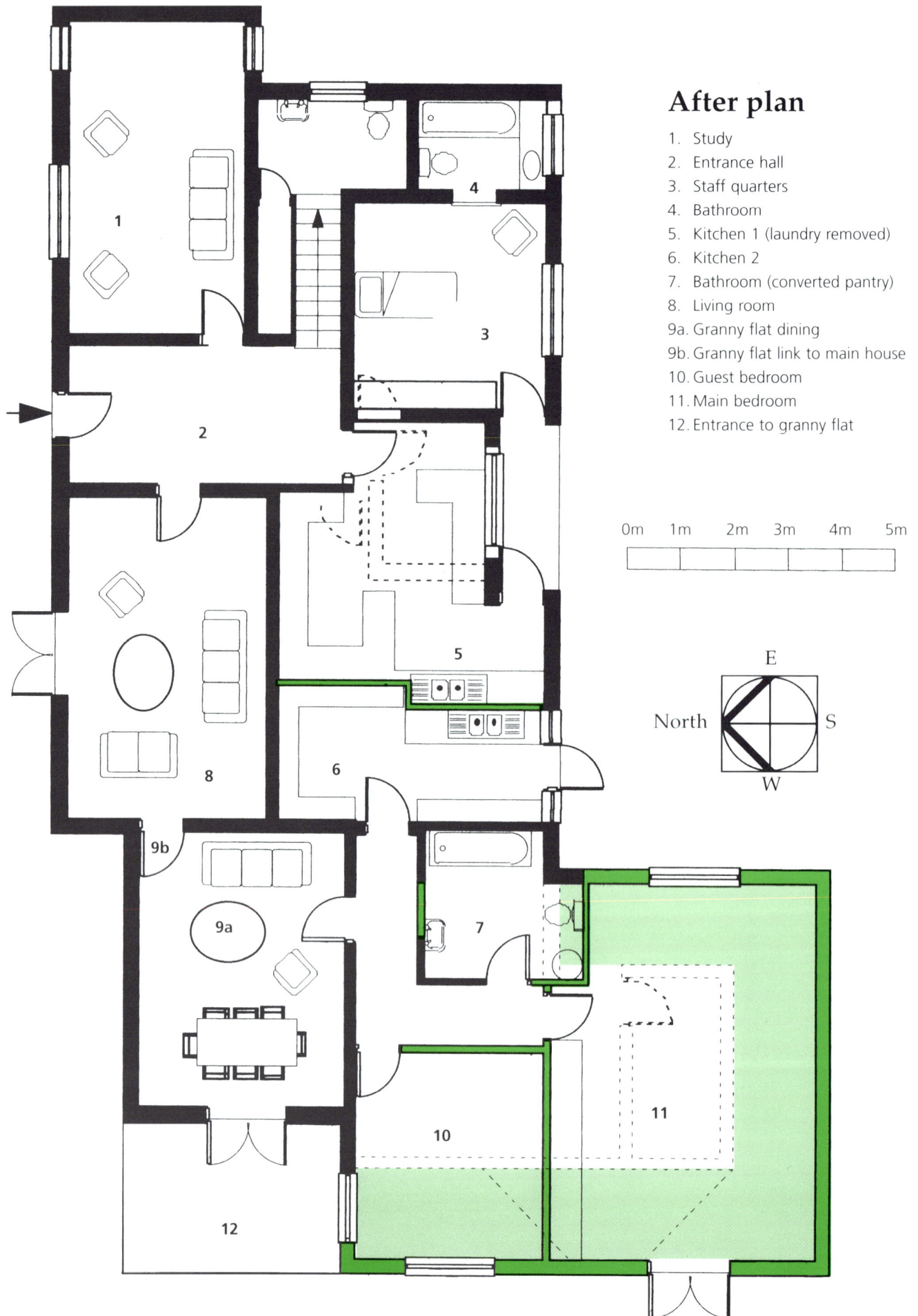

PLAN 7

After plan

1. Study
2. Entrance hall
3. Staff quarters
4. Bathroom
5. Kitchen 1 (laundry removed)
6. Kitchen 2
7. Bathroom (converted pantry)
8. Living room
9a. Granny flat dining
9b. Granny flat link to main house
10. Guest bedroom
11. Main bedroom
12. Entrance to granny flat

0m 1m 2m 3m 4m 5m

E
North S
W

A family holiday home was given a completely new internal layout and an upstairs playroom. Bedrooms were added and the living spaces were transferred to the sunny side of the house. These now lead to a covered patio where there is a built-in braai. A new double garage with a door to the covered entrance walkway and staff quarters were also added.

The altered home's entrance is clearly defined from the street with a pergola-covered walkway leading to the front door, past a newly gravelled courtyard and pond.

The long central passage was opened up to the new courtyard on one side and the large rooms were converted into slightly smaller separate bedrooms.

The main bedroom is located at the corner of the house with a corner window opening up the space to views. It has its own en-suite bathroom and private courtyard with outdoor shower. All of the bedrooms and living spaces have sliding doors leading onto a front patio. Similarly, the new upstairs playroom leads to its own balcony.

A walled yard was also added.

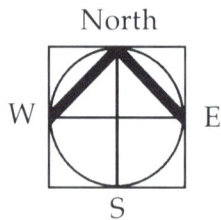

Before plan

1. Garage
2. Staff quarters
3. WC
4. Store
5. Living area
6. Bathroom
7. Store
8. Bedroom
9. Bathroom
10. Bedroom
11. Kitchen
12. Bedroom
13. Split-level lounge/dining area, with doors to patio

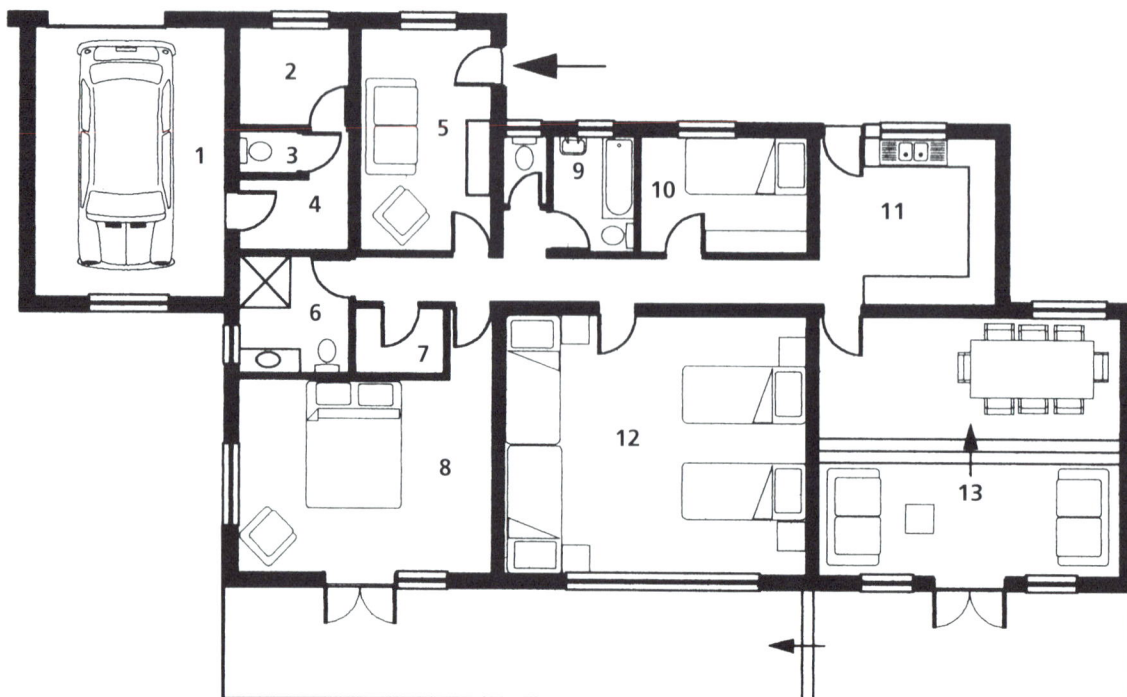

After plan

1. Patio/braai area
2. Yard
3. Kitchen
4. Open-plan lounge/dining area
5. WC
6. Courtyard with pond
7. New double garage
8. Covered entrance walkway
9. Bathroom
10. Bathroom
11. Courtyard
12. Main bedroom (steps removed) and floor made level
13. Bedroom
14. Bedroom
15. Patio (one level of steps removed)

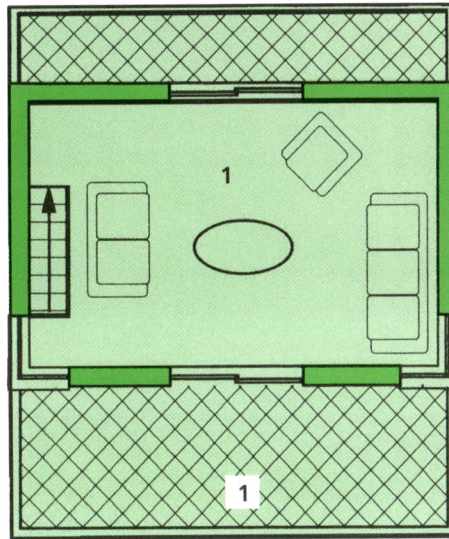

After plan of upper floor

1. Playroom, with corner windows and sliding doors to balconies

0m 1m 2m 3m 4m 5m

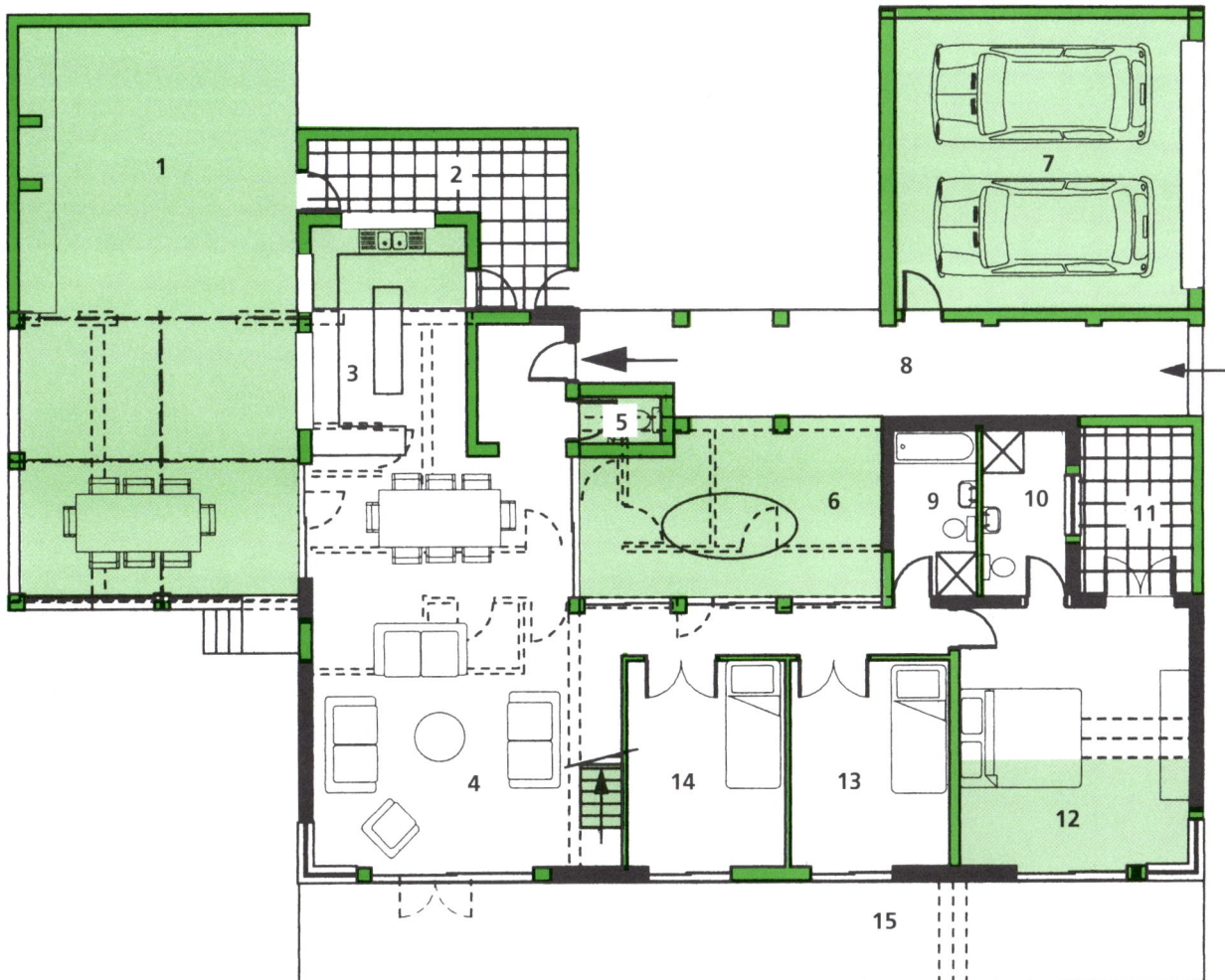

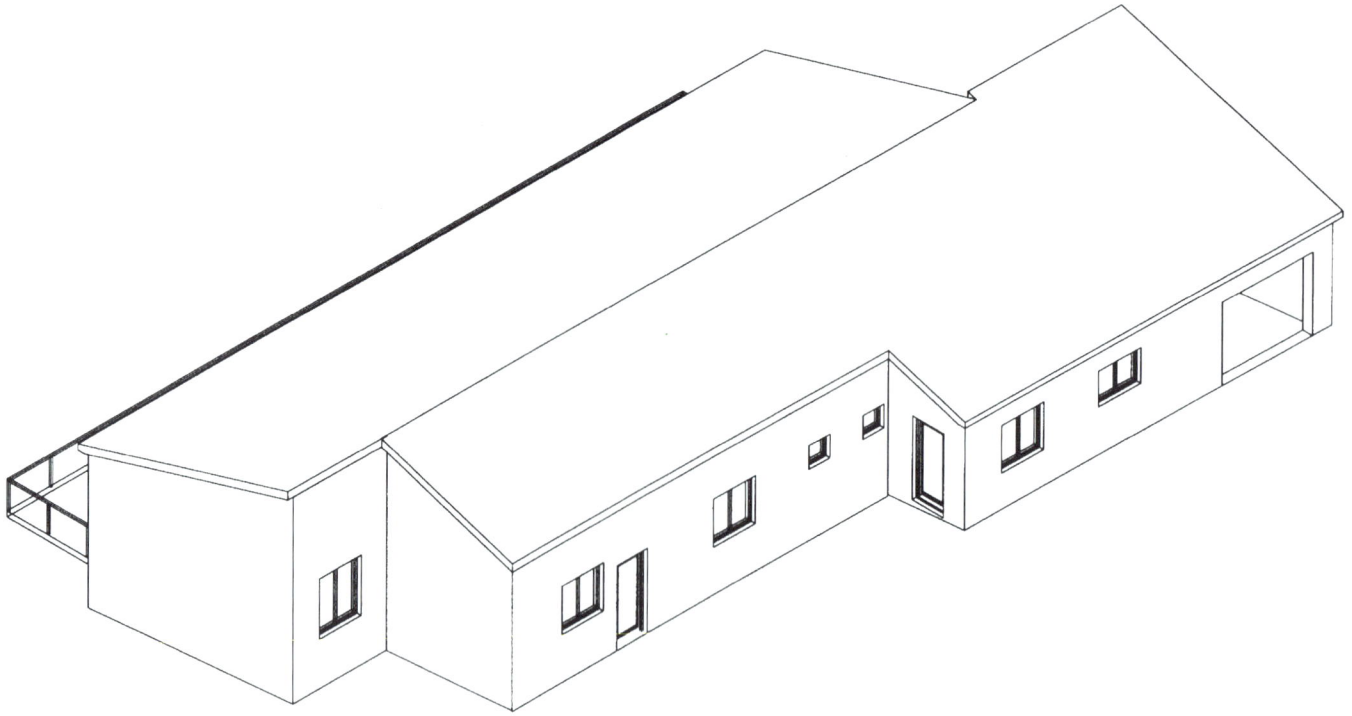

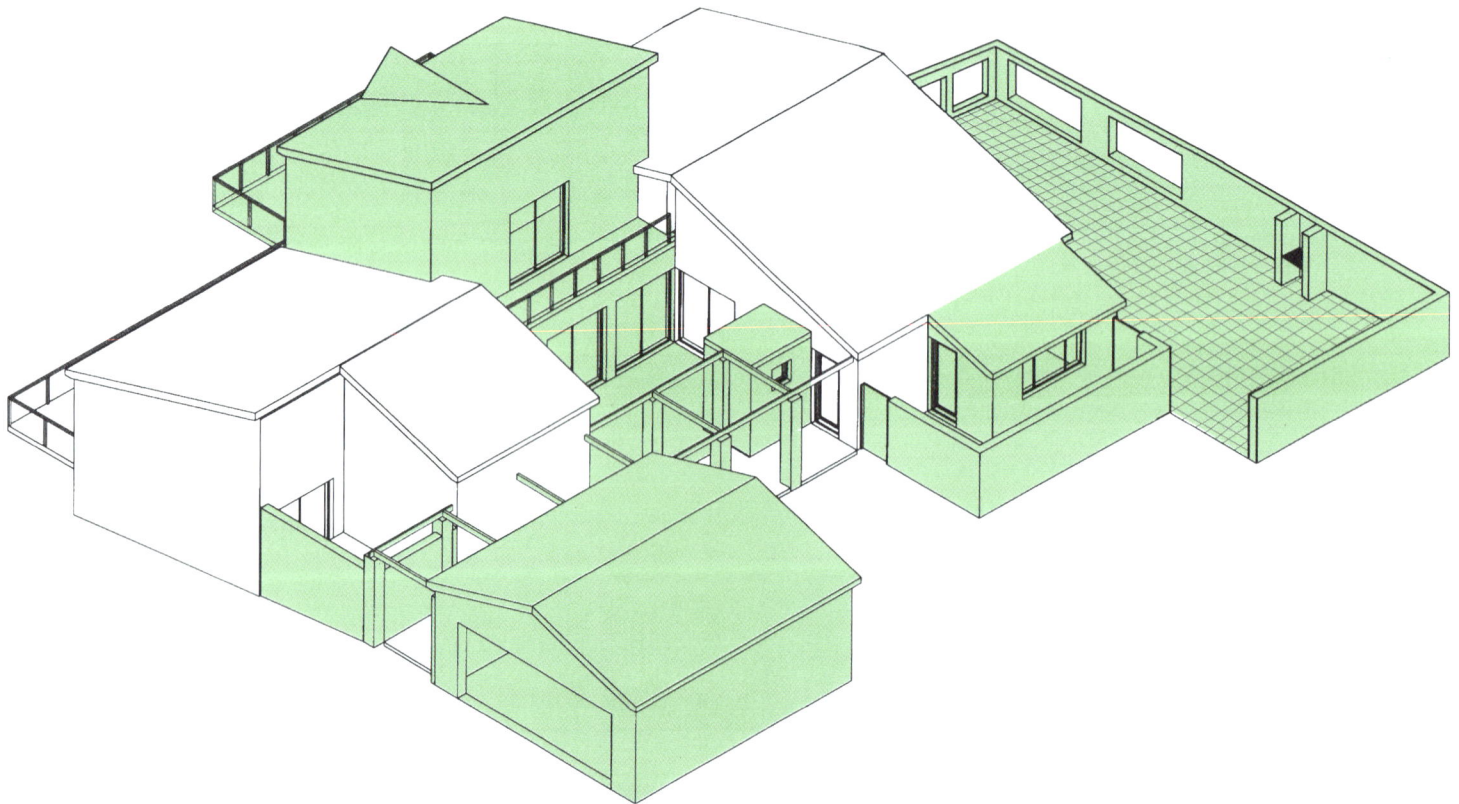

CONVERTING UNUSED SPACE

If you need more space but are unable to extend the existing boundaries of your home, consider extending into the attic or basement, or converting an existing outbuilding. Conversions are usually less expensive than new additions since they do not require foundations or new walls.

ATTIC

The attic may have enough ceiling height to be used as it is, or your roof could be raised and dormer windows added to create the required heights and to allow for natural light and ventilation. An attic room will need to be insulated for heat and cold and made weather-tight.

BASEMENT

If the basement is not too damp and the ceiling height is high enough, it could be converted into a workshop, hobby room, garage, wine cellar or guest suite if you can provide adequate light and ventilation.

OUTBUILDINGS

Outbuildings such as garages, staff quarters, stables or laundries can also be converted to different uses.

VERANDAHS AND BALCONIES

Verandahs and balconies can be enclosed to extend an existing room or to create a new room, bathroom or study. These spaces are often too narrow to be used as bedrooms and you will need to consider the light and ventilation effects on rooms off the existing balcony.

CHECKLIST FOR CONVERSIONS

HEADROOM
Check the building regulations to determine the necessary headroom. This is usually a minimum of 2,4 m for 'habitable spaces', such as bedrooms, kitchens and living rooms, and a minimum of 2,1 m for bathrooms and stores.

DAYLIGHT AND VENTILATION
According to the building regulations, habitable spaces require an opening (window, skylight, etc.) measuring a minimum of 10% of the floor area for natural light and 5% of the floor area for natural ventilation.

CIRCULATION
This refers to the way the converted space is accessed from the existing house (stairs, covered passages or walkways).

ZONING
What will the converted space be used for and how does this relate to the adjacent spaces? For example, it is not a good idea to place a quiet bedroom directly off a noisy living space or to locate a toilet directly off a kitchen, without a separating lobby space.

SERVICES
Do you want electricity, water supply and drainage in the space? How will these factors be linked to existing services?

WEATHER RESISTANCE
The existing space may need to be insulated (especially attics), damp may need to be attended to and remedied (usually in basements and in garages).

EXTERIOR APPEARANCE
New windows and doors may be necessary to light and ventilate the spaces and for access. The effect of these on the overall appearance of your home needs to be considered.

STRUCTURE
This is a very important consideration as it affects your building costs. Even if the structure is sound, the additional loads of, say, an attic space, or the added depth of a basement, may mean that the existing structure will need to be reinforced or underpinned. Your architect and engineer will be able to advise you on this.

BASEMENTS

Not many South African homes are built with basements, but sometimes, due to the slope of the property, there is unused space below a home which is not difficult to convert to usable space, providing there is sufficient headroom. Many older homes were raised above the ground with small storage and cellar spaces. These inevitably became unused, dark and dank. Generally, these spaces are considered best for storage and housing a wine cellar as the temperature remains relatively constant. However, this valuable space could be put to better use.

It can be successfully converted into a separate rentable space, a workshop, a photographic darkroom, a laundry or staff quarters if you do not want a direct connection to the main house. Alternatively, you could improve the relationship between your house and garden, which is usually at basement level, by creating an internal stairway link between the house and the basement. It could also be converted into additional living space or a garage depending on its accessibility to a driveway.

Basement conversions may require existing floor levels to be lowered to create enough headroom. The existing house footings will have to be underpinned if the excavations expose these footings. If excavation works are necessary, it is essential that you consult a structural engineer.

Other considerations are:

- access to the basement area;
- light;
- ventilation; and
- sufficient height in the rooms according to regulations.

Damp is often a problem which needs to be treated before making basement spaces habitable and this work needs to be carried out by specialists. Living in a damp room is very unpleasant and unhealthy.

ATTICS

If the roof of your house is pitched (not flat) you have what is known as an attic or loft. If the pitch is high enough and you can stand comfortably in the roof space, you could use this valuable area for additional rooms and for accessing views of your surroundings through roof windows.

Creating a usable attic space not only provides a special type of habitable space, it can enhance and alter the external character of the home as the roof is a visible aesthetic factor. Whether your home is part of a terrace, detached or semi-detached, you need to consider the effect of attic windows on neighbouring buildings. You may even need to obtain special permission from the conservation unit of your local authority to install the windows if your home is of particular architectural or historic merit.

Attic conversions are not as simple as they appear because you need to consider the existing roof structure, local authority restrictions, and the effect on your neighbours. The existing roof space often houses the hot-water cylinder, electric cables and the chimney stack, and these may need to be altered if you plan to make maximum use of the area.

If you plan to make any structural alterations to your roof to create the space you need, you will need to consult an architect and possibly a structural engineer. There are some building companies that can offer a combined design-and-build service and are worth investigating. Since the conversion of an attic space can greatly affect the external appearance of your home, we suggest you ask an architect to prepare a sketch drawing to confirm its appearance and the options available.

If you do not have the required headroom and the existing roof space cannot easily be converted, you can still create an open feeling within your home by removing the ceiling, exposing the roof timbers and adding a gallery-type space in the roof. The gallery can overlook the room and add a useful sleeping deck or library to your living area. When opening up an attic space in this manner, you increase the feeling of height in the room below.

CHECKLIST FOR ATTIC CONVERSIONS
- Do you need to alter the existing roof structure extensively to create usable space in which you can stand and walk?
- Does the existing space lend itself easily to complying with local authority regulations for heights for habitable rooms and party walls between neighbours for fire safety?
- Is there existing ground-floor-level space that can be used for a staircase to the attic?
- Can the existing structure carry the additional weight of an attic conversion?
- Can building take place out of the rainy season? At some point the roof will need to be opened to install windows. This could mean that your home is at the mercy of the elements for some time.

If these points are carefully considered, you have the opportunity to create a very comfortable space inside your roof, which could have special alcove-type windows and sloped ceilings which give interesting shape and character to the rooms. One could create a balcony at roof level and enjoy the views without raising the height of your home.

Some attic conversions require the existing roof space to be raised to achieve the regulation headroom height. Raising the existing roof space often means that the timber roof structure needs to be altered and separated from the original ceiling structure which usually makes up a roof truss.

ELEMENTS OF AN ATTIC CONVERSION
Access stairs
Stairs take up more space than you may realise – particularly if you want them to be comfortable to walk up and down. Generally, a comfortable step is a height of not more than 200 mm, a length (tread) of not less than 260 mm, with the width of the stair being not less than 1 m. One alternative is a ladder-type access; another is an extendible

loft ladder which can be pushed up and pulled down as required and does not disturb the space below when it is not in use. These two options are the best if you only wish to use the attic space for storage. Spiral stairs are also useful if space is limited, and closed, single-length stairs or steps with a landing half-way allow you to utilise the space below the stairs for storage. Another option is to leave the timber treads open so that light filters through to the space below. This could be used as a place for bookcases, wine storage or for locating a telephone. Steps can be made of timber, concrete or steel, depending on your requirements, the cost and the style you want to achieve. Spiral stairs can come as ready-made metal structures, but you will need to consider base and top supports.

The location of your access stair is important as there needs to be sufficient headroom at the top of the steps (2 m minimum) which usually means that the stair needs to enter the attic somewhere near the middle of the roof where the space is at its highest. You may need to create a raised roof section to accommodate the stair access and avoid bumping one's head.

Heights in habitable attic rooms

The National Building Regulations recommend a minimum height for habitable attic rooms of 2,4 m over a minimum area of 6 m². If the space does not meet this requirement, there are various solutions, such as lowering the ceiling of the rooms below to create the required height or raising the roof slightly. These are expensive options and should be avoided unless absolutely necessary. Additional flat ceiling area may be created by adding more dormer window spaces. Exposing the roof structure and placing the new ceiling between the roof beams, or slightly altering the roof truss without altering the roof itself (for example, by raising the height of the tie beam with guidance from an engineer), can also increase the finished height of your attic room. The side spaces where the height is restricted make useful storage areas and cupboards. Areas where the headroom is not suitable for habitable rooms can be used for bathrooms and storage.

Windows

The inclusion of windows in the attic conversion is critical if adequate light and ventilation are to be created. Attic insulation is very important as this space originally formed the only insulating barrier between the roof and the rooms below, and it can get very hot inside. The type of window you decide to use affects the style and use of the attic space. The simplest and most economical windows to install are rooflights which follow the angle of the roof line. These can be fixed or opened. The disadvantage of these windows is that they do not create the added height and alcove-type space of a dormer window. However they are options to be considered and can be carefully positioned so that you still get a good view out. They will need sun protection (blinds) to prevent the space becoming too hot. Dormer windows are normally used for attic conversions. They have a

wonderful way of connecting you to the outside and creating alcoves and special window areas. Dormer windows should be made high enough to stand in and have windows that can open wide. Types of dormer window include the inverted dormer window style which is set back into the roof to form a balcony (*see* illustrations). Although inverted dormer windows create valuable outdoor space, they need to be carefully waterproofed to prevent leakage into the rooms below.

In a gable-ended house, the end walls can be opened to provide light and air to the attic space. When positioning dormer windows in your attic space, you need to consider not only their exterior appearance but also the views you overlook and the prevailing wind direction.

Floors

Besides structural considerations, you also need to be aware of sound transference from attic floors to the rooms below. The support system was originally designed to carry only a ceiling and will need to be strengthened. As the floors are usually made of timber, you will have to consider noise, the creaking of loose boards, etc. This problem can be solved by using larger sized boarding rather than strip timber floors, and using carpets with thick underlays which absorb sound. The spacing of existing roof supports will probably need to be increased to support the floorboards, and additional timber beams will be required between the existing roof trusses to support the new floors. Although about 40% of the floor area of an attic cannot be used due to the lack of headroom, it is wise to take the flooring to the limits of the space to allow the low sides to be used for built-in cupboards and storage.

Walls and ceilings

It is usual to fix a plasterboard layer to the existing timber roof-support system to create walls and ceilings. Insulation is needed behind these layers. It is wise to choose a thick plasterboard for the walls so that pictures, built-in furniture or bathroom accessories can be hung on them. Walls and ceilings can also be made of timber which, though more expensive, is aesthetically pleasing.

Insulation

To keep the attic space warm and to conserve heat in winter, and to maintain a cool space in summer, it is essential to insulate the walls and the ceiling. To help control moisture formation, the space between the finished inside room and the outside roofing should be ventilated and a vapour barrier installed. Moisture inside this space can lead to the deterioration of the roof structure. In summer the attic space becomes hot and it is sometimes necessary to provide extractor fans. Positioning dormer windows on opposite sides of the room will allow for cross ventilation and keep the space cool.

Existing services

If you plan to add a bathroom in your attic conversion, try to locate it above an existing bathroom so that you can use the same sewer drainage/vent pipe. Hot- and cold-water supplies will also be easy to extend.

GARAGES AND OUTBUILDINGS

Outbuildings that are either separate or attached to your home are sources for conversion and extension. These spaces are often derelict or unused and can be easily converted to extend your home or provide staff quarters, a guest room, a laundry, a children's playroom or a home office. You need to consider the proportions of these spaces as single garages are often just too narrow for use as comfortable living spaces. Minor changes, such as adding bay windows or pop-out extensions, can make these relatively narrow spaces wide enough to live in.

An often-asked question is whether it is possible to build a guest suite on top of a garage. Here, one needs to check the town planning regulations for your area as there are usually specific height restrictions for buildings located on site boundaries. This is where outbuildings are most often located. You need to consider not only the cost implications of such a proposal but also its effect on the neighbourhood.

It is important when converting an outbuilding to make it seem similar to the main house style in both appearance and proportion. If you want the outbuilding to be linked to the main house, this needs to be carefully considered so that it does not appear out of place. You need to think about how the height of the outbuilding relates to your main house roof height and either link it comfortably to the main house roof or fit the connection underneath, without disturbing the existing structure. The floor levels of the main house and their relation to the outbuilding's floor level will also have to be considered carefully. This will determine whether you will need to build steps or raise the floor level.

The old Cape style of linking outbuildings was by low white walls. Links such as covered walkways, pergolas, garden paths and special plantings can also integrate buildings on a property.

Be careful not to lose garage facilities as these are useful spaces for protecting motor cars, storage and for a messy workshop. If it is feasible to convert the existing garage, try to recreate this important function elsewhere on the property and possibly create an undercover link to the main house for security and weather reasons. It is often necessary to have secure access from the street to your home and this can be achieved by installing remote control garage doors and/or driveway gates.

Outbuildings make very good places from which to run a small business as they are secure but separate from the main house. You will have to check the property's title deeds to see if there are any restrictions on changing the use of an outbuilding. You will also need to check the zoning of the property with your local authority. If the zoning is for single residential, you will need to confirm any regulations on adding a living space. Approval may be granted if the space is called a granny flat or staff quarters as these are permissible without going through the complicated procedure of re-zoning the property.

The local authorities are rethinking their regulations on density on properties and the current trend is to allow for more densification in residential areas to alleviate the housing shortage.

However, the existing legislation applicable to these conversions is still in place and it is recommended that you consult your architect for advice on the regulations related to the proposed change and to complete the work with authority approval.

PLAN 9

This home was rearranged to allow for better flow between the rooms. The front door was moved and a useless passage space was lost.

A television room was added in a large living space with doors leading to the enclosed verandah. Sliding doors were installed between the television room and the living space. This allows for the rooms to be opened up to create a large entertainment space leading to the verandah if required. An en-suite bathroom was added to the main bedroom and an enclosed side verandah was turned into a study area off this room. An odd-shaped bedroom was enlarged.

The kitchen was repositioned off the dining space, with a back door leading to the alley. The original kitchen became a bedroom. Glazed sliding doors separate the kitchen from the dining area allowing light through the spaces.

Before plan

1. Study
2. Kitchen
3. Living/dining area
4. Entrance patio
5. Bathroom
6. Bedroom
7. Bedroom
8. Bedroom
9. Enclosed stoep

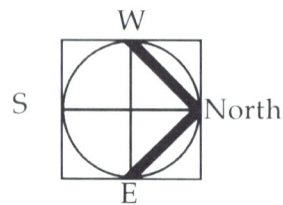

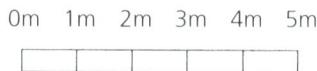

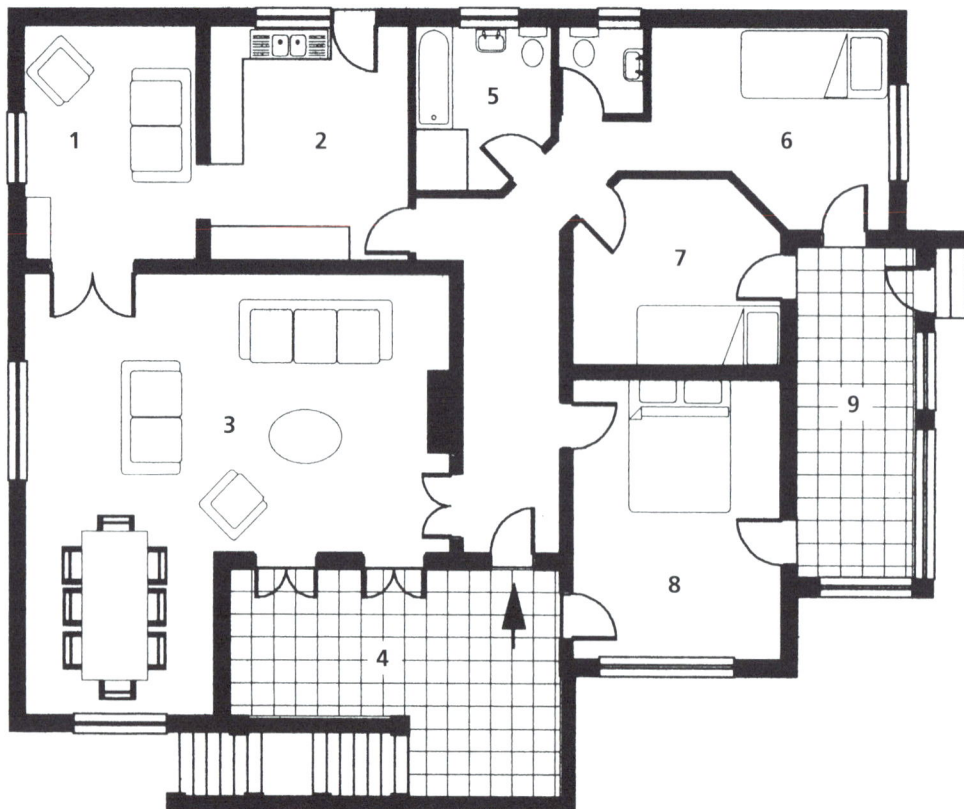

0m   1m   2m   3m   4m   5m

After plan

1. New kitchen, with doors to back yard
2. Bedroom (original kitchen)
3a. New living/dining area, with sliding doors to TV room and doors from dining area to patio
3b. TV room, with doors to patio
4. Entrance patio
5. Bathroom
6. Enlarged bedroom
7. Bathroom
8. Bedroom
9. Study

The high roof space available in this home was converted into a main bedroom, a dressing room and a bathroom, adding needed room space to the main house without extending onto the small plot. The new extension affords an unexpected mountain view. Due to the slope of the roof, the lower side spaces were easily converted into useful storage and clothes cupboards.

The added bathroom with shower, washbasin and toilet fitted into a newly created dormer window space. Two other dormer windows extended the main bedroom space, allowing a nook for a reading desk and built-in seating area with inward-opening doors and a railing, looking towards the mountain view. The new timber boarded floor was made up of large size boards and covered with a heavy carpet and underfelt to muffle noise and avoid the inevitable creaking boards that come with timber strip-flooring on upper levels. The new room is accessed by a generous spiral stair leading from a downstairs passage, allowing the opening up of a kitchen space in the original home.

The appearance of the original house was maintained and enhanced by the added dormer windows which were finished with the same roofing material as the main roof.

The attic was well insulated against heat and cold, and a roof extractor was added to remove any hot air build-up which normally occurs in these spaces. The original hot-water cylinder has been neatly relocated in the lower, unusable spaces of the attic and is accessible through a panel in the built-in cupboards. The original electric cables were recessed into the roof truss tie beams and covered with the new floor boarding. Timber beams were added between the trusses to support the new floorboards.

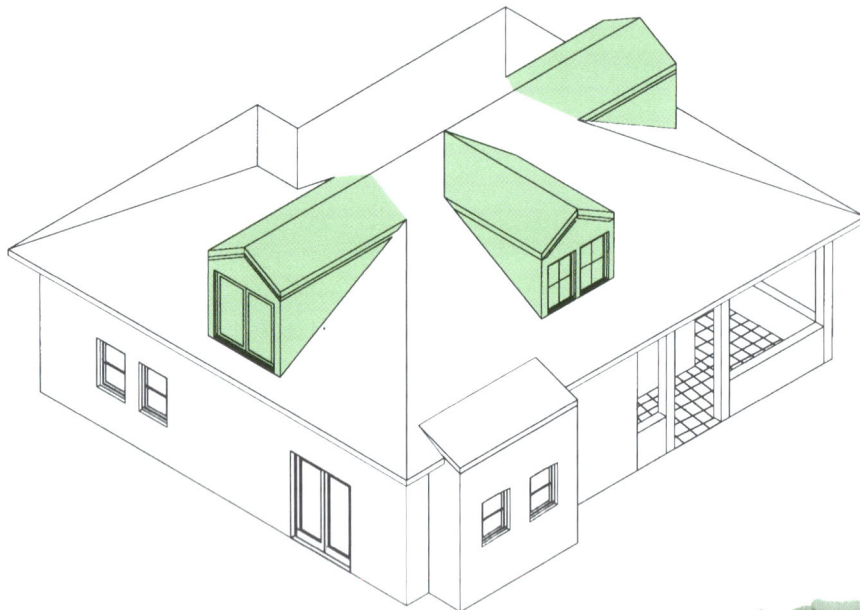

Ground level plan

1. Living/dining area
2. Kitchen
3. Spiral staircase
4. Bathroom
5. Bedroom
6. Bedroom
7. Verandah

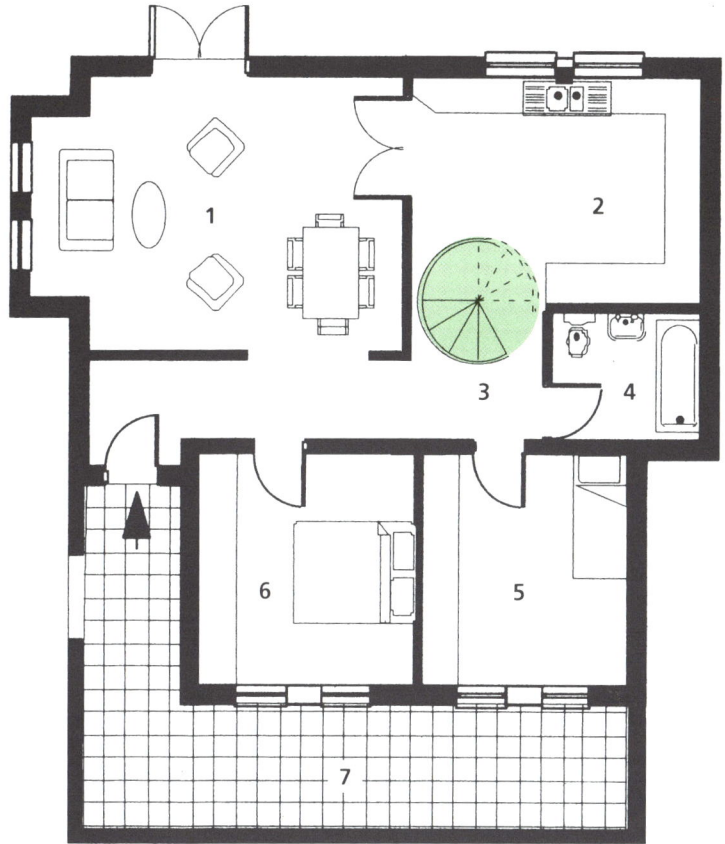

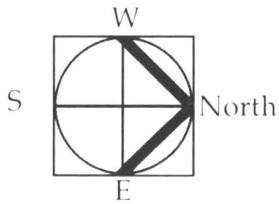

Attic level plan

1. Window seat
2. Roof (original remaining)
3. Spiral staircase
4. Attic bedroom
5. Bathroom, with shower
6. Dressing room

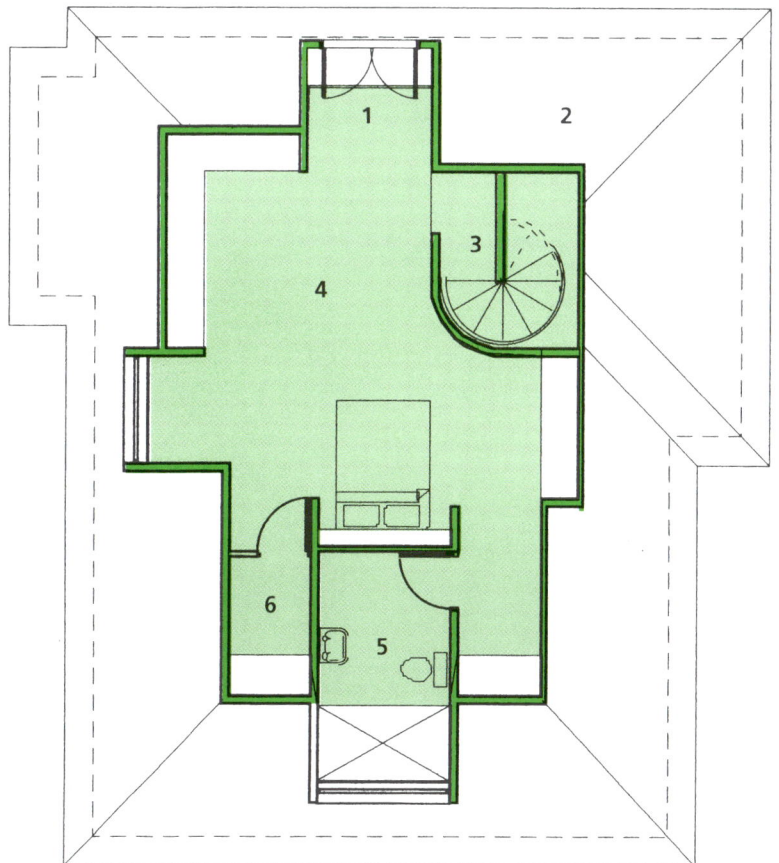

The back of this home faced a magnificent view and there were problems with the flow to an existing garden and swimming pool area. The kitchen and bathroom, both of which were in need of upgrading, had small, north-facing windows and the kitchen had a small balcony leading to a steep stairway to the swimming pool area. The flow from the inside to the outside was limited and a damp, unusable basement could only be reached from the pool garden area.

There were two medium-sized bedrooms in the house and a small bedroom. From the front door there was a view along the passage to a blank wall. The extensive alterations turned the property into a stylish family home with a large upper level patio, a basement kitchen and 360 degree views.

The existing kitchen and bathroom were demolished and relocated so that the end of the house could be opened up into a large living space leading to the patio.

The dark and dingy basement was excavated to give additional headroom and converted into an open-plan kitchen/dining area with French doors leading to the pool garden area. A nook was left as a laundry area.

The basement is reached by a new staircase leading from the lounge area. The stair treads were lined with oregon pine boards to match the original pine floors in the main house.

The small bedroom was enlarged and windows were added to the space, and a central room was converted into a guest bedroom with an en-suite bathroom. A separate guest suite leading off the pool area was upgraded.

Before upper-level plan

1. Roof of guest suite
2. Study
3. Kitchen
4. Dining room
5. Room over garage
6. Lounge
7. Bedroom
8. Bedroom
9. Main bedroom

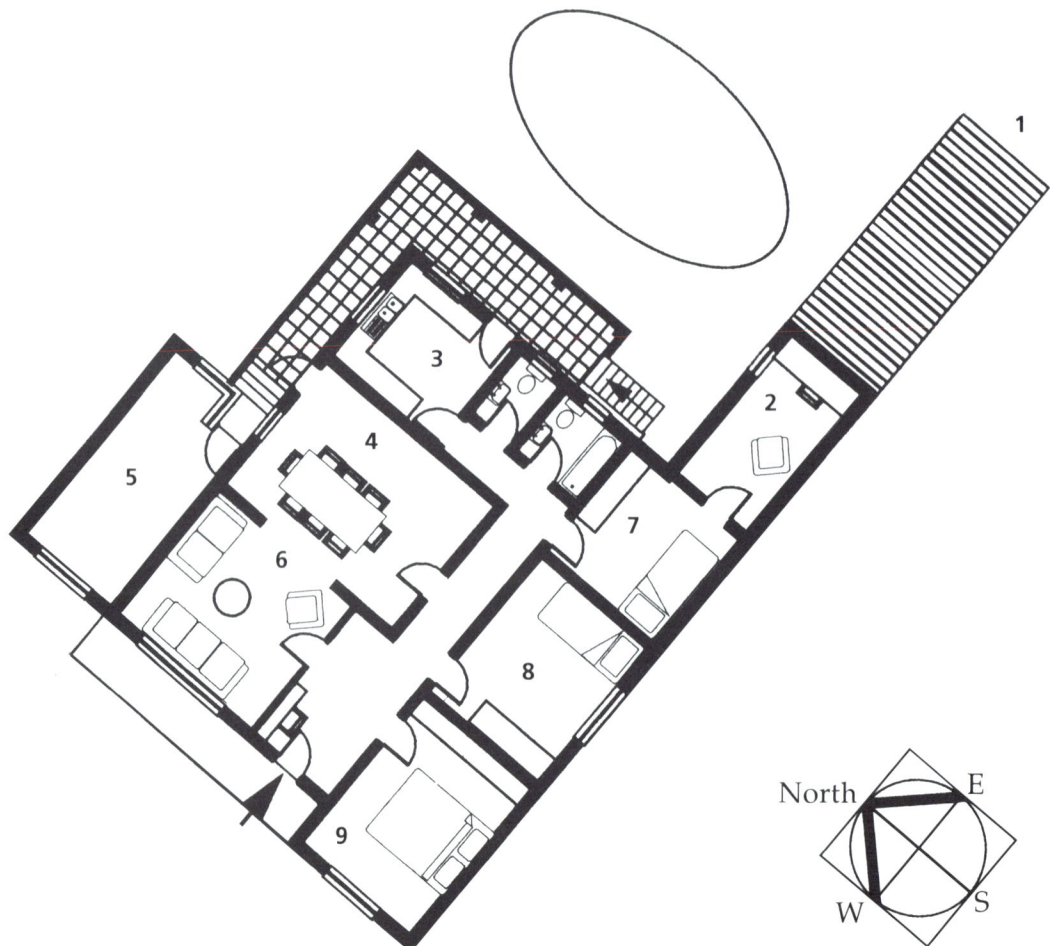

0m 1m 2m 3m 4m 5m

After basement plan

1. Guest room
2. Bathroom
3. Store
4. WC and shower
5. Kitchen/dining area, with doors
   to yard and garden

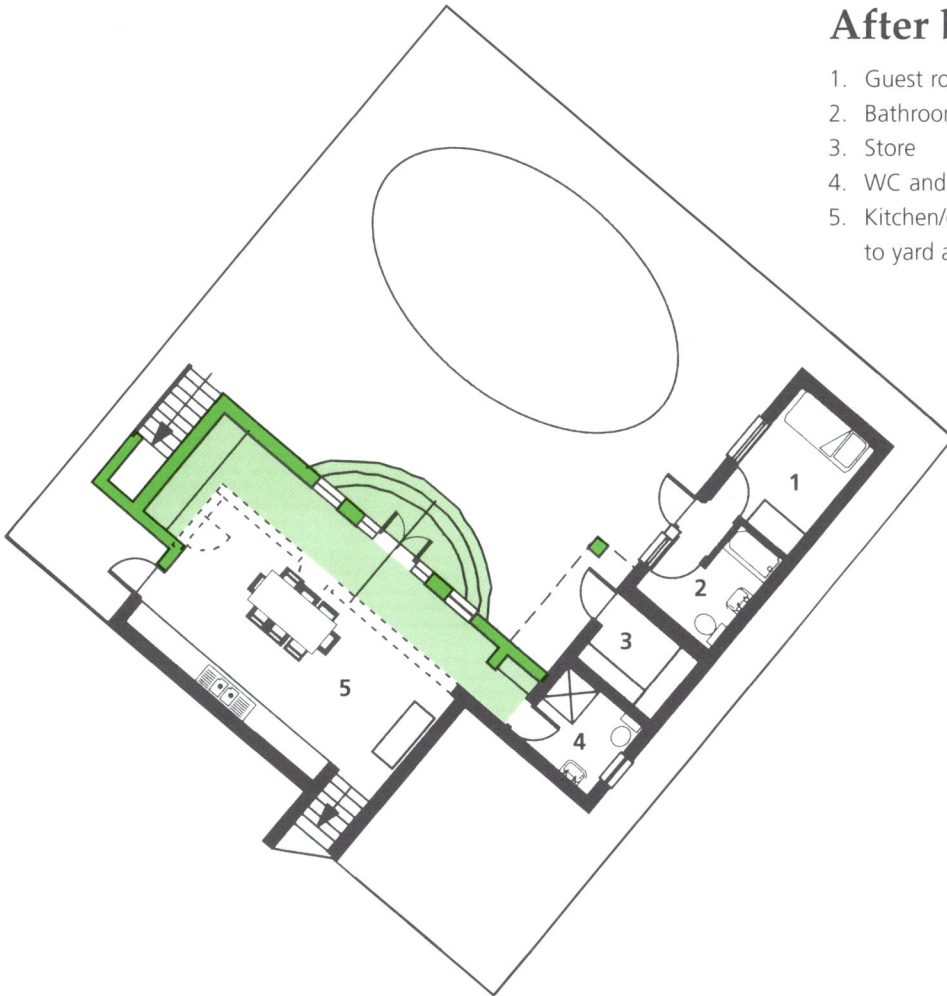

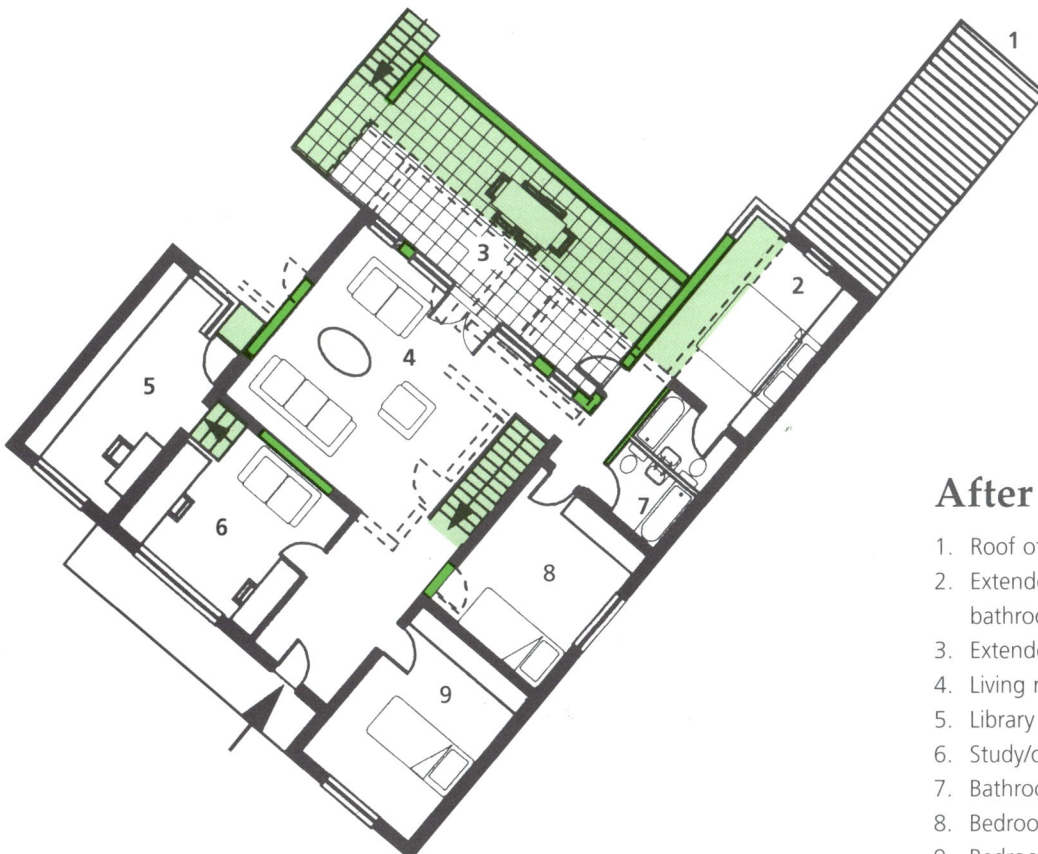

After upper-level plan

1. Roof of guest suite
2. Extended main bedroom, with en-suite
   bathroom
3. Extended patio
4. Living room, with doors to patio
5. Library (over garage) with access to study
6. Study/office
7. Bathroom
8. Bedroom
9. Bedroom

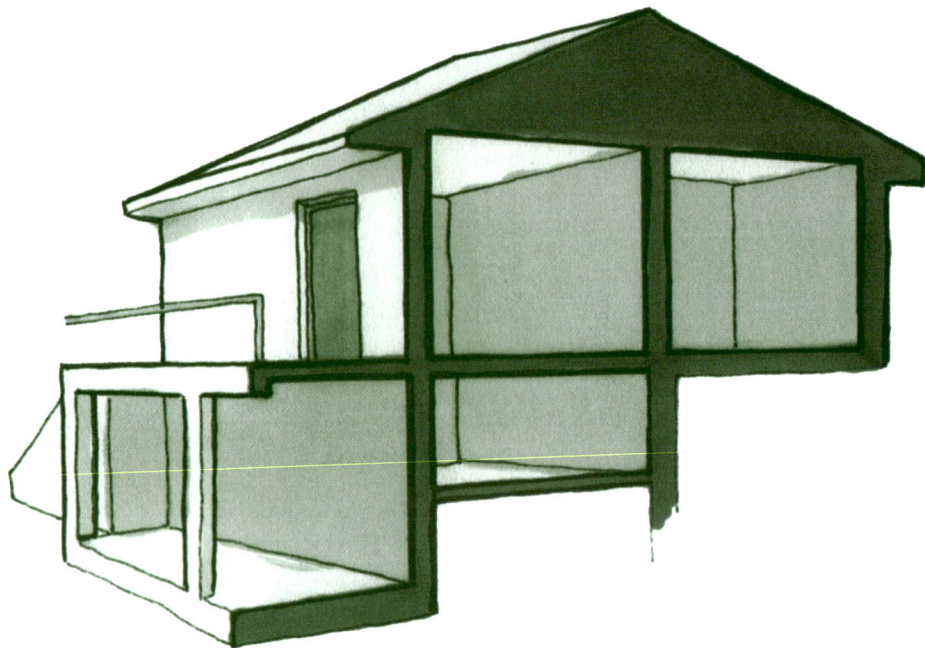

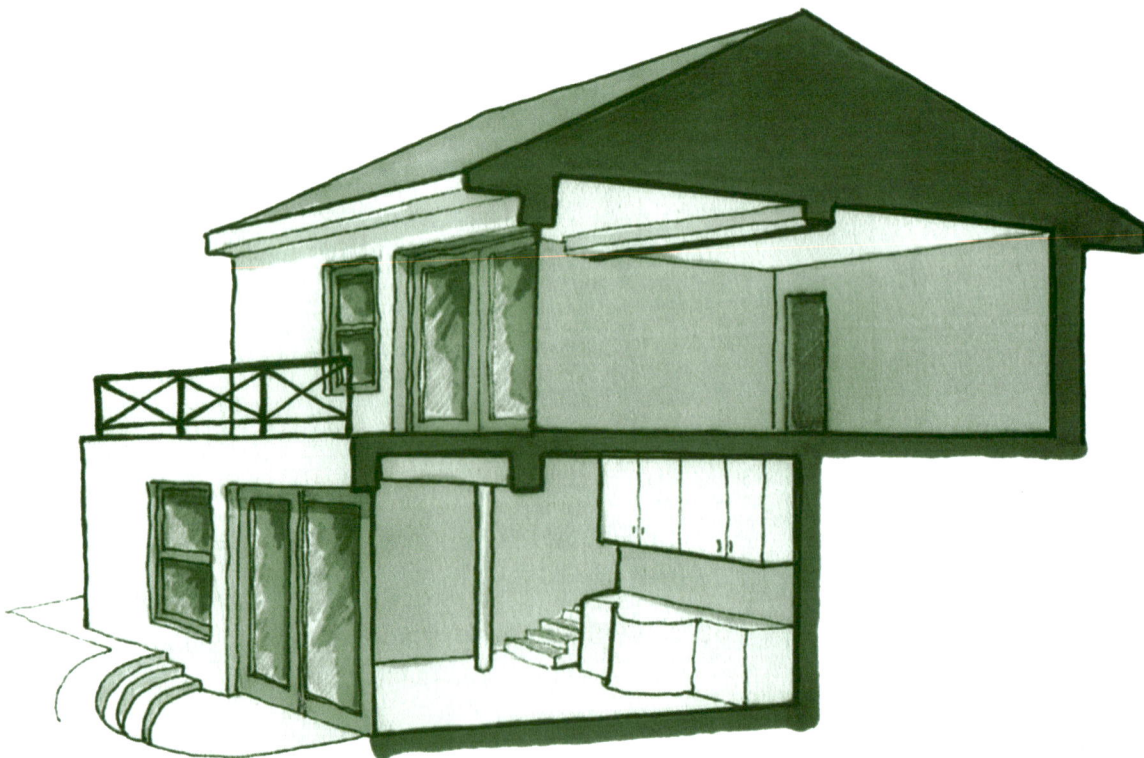

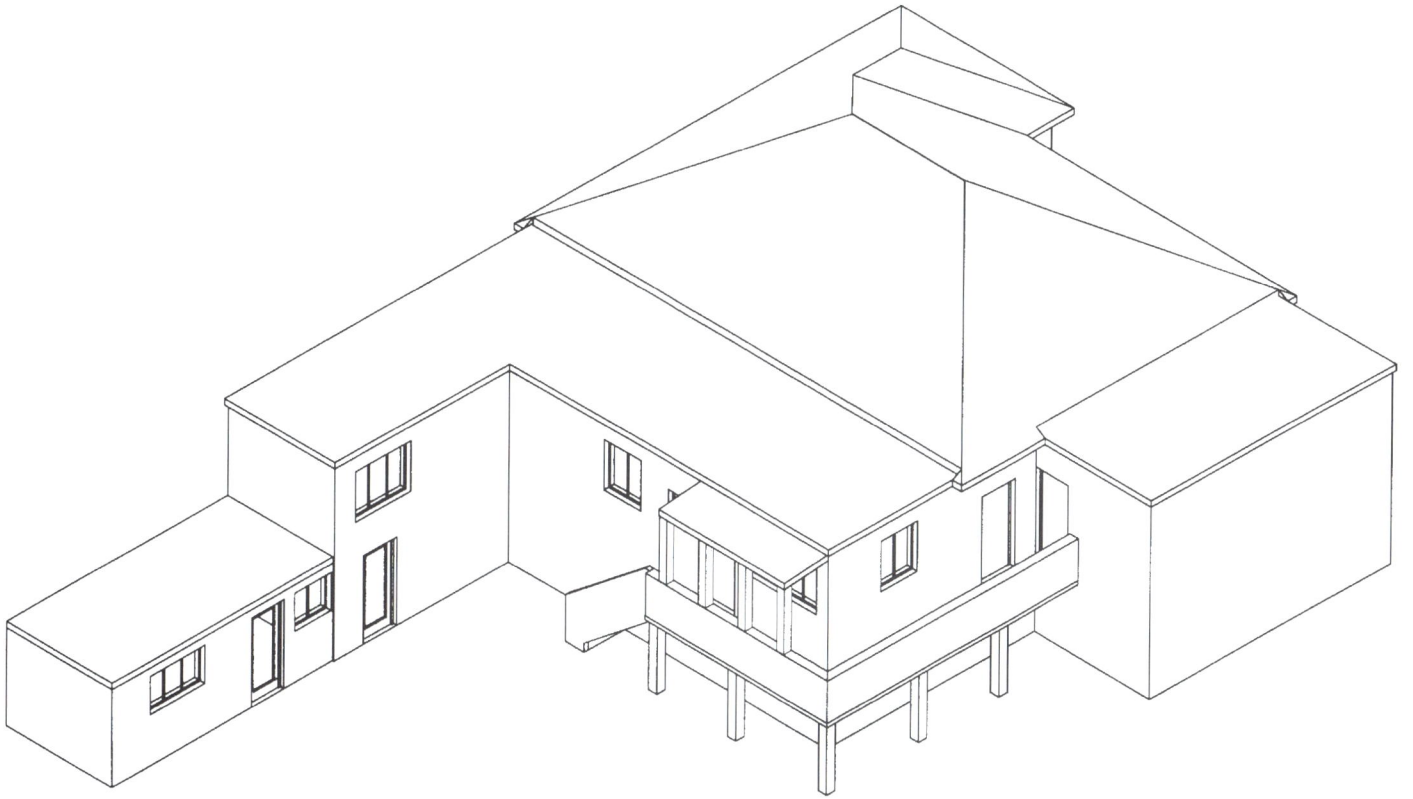

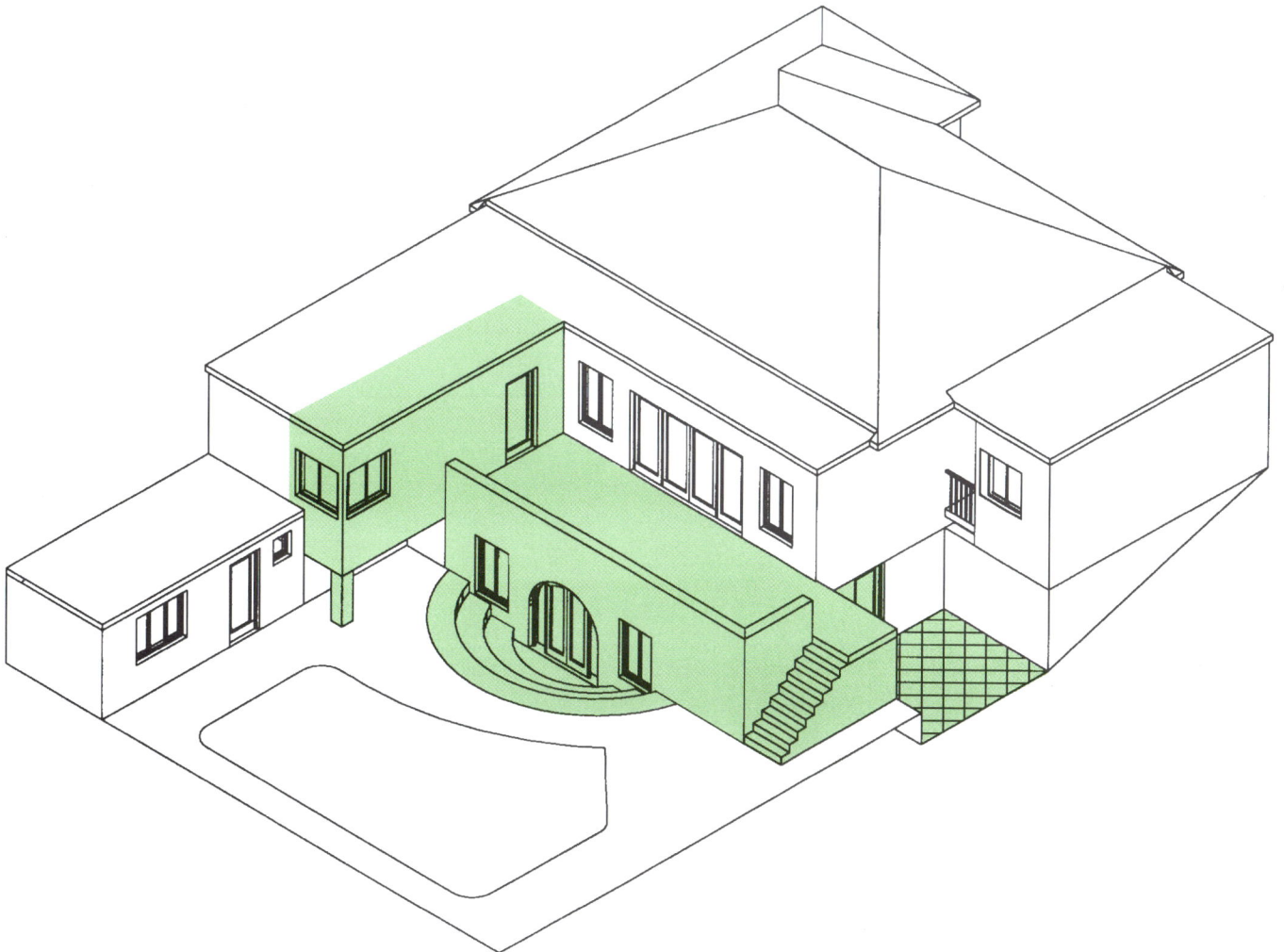

A dark basement store and staff quarters were converted into a two-bedroom granny flat with its own access from two sides. The dark back room was given a facelift when space was created by excavating a courtyard off this room. A spiral staircase is located in the courtyard, giving access to the street level above. The new glazed doors leading from the second bedroom to the private courtyard add light and space.

The new main bedroom now has a dressing room and an en-suite bathroom.

The existing kitchen space was made open-plan to a living/dining area and a fireplace was added for warmth in winter.

Access to the basement level is mainly from a back street, and a carport, patio and swimming pool were added to the small garden created at the lower level.

0m 1m 2m 3m 4m 5m

Before plan

1. Outside WC
2. Bathroom
3. Staff bedroom
4. Living room
5. Kitchen
6. Store space

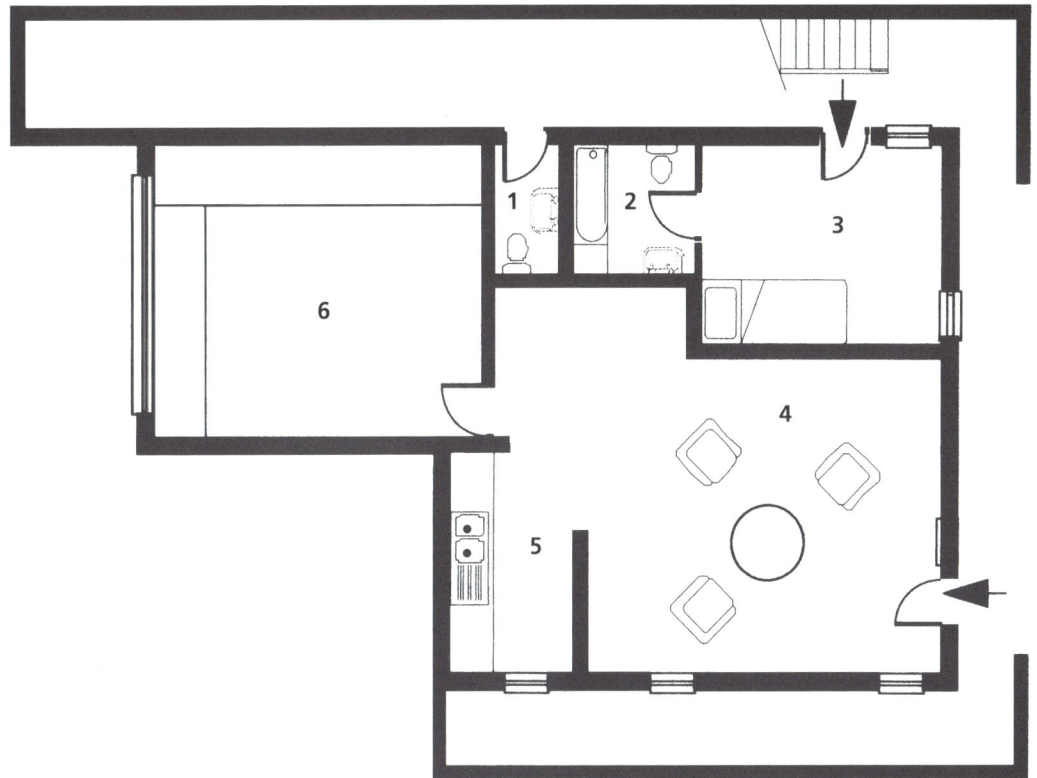

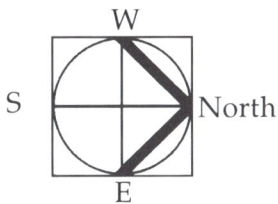

W

S   North

E

After plan

1. En-suite bathroom
2. Dressing room
3. Main bedroom, with doors
   to patio
4. Living/dining room, with new
   fireplace and doors to patio
5. Open-plan kitchen
6. New bedroom, with doors
   to courtyard
7. Bathroom
8. Stairs to upper level
9. Courtyard
10. Patio

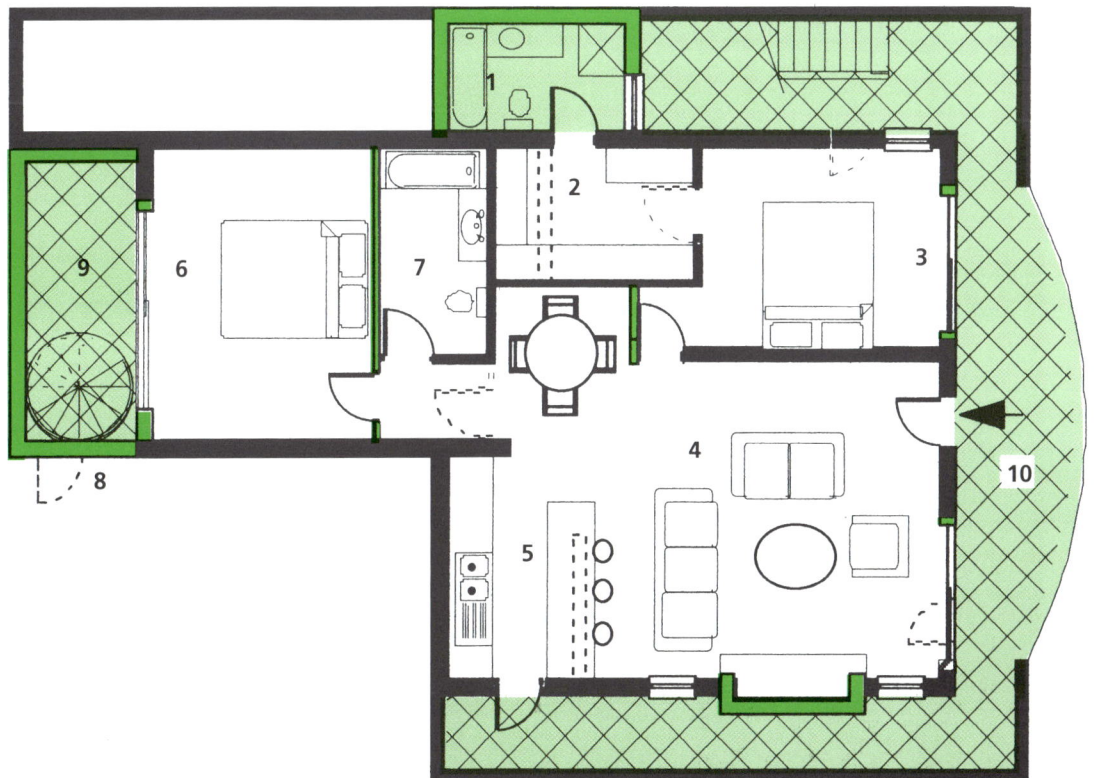

A single garage with staff quarters below was extended to become a four-car garage/workshop with granny flat/pool room below. A swimming pool was added to the back area of this property. The site extends between two access roads and slopes dramatically. A separate pedestrian access from the street level garage to the property was added and this is entered from the side of the garage and from the street. This has created a secure access for the owners, and visitors can enter the property without having to go through the garage. The feel of this back space was enhanced and the family pool room was extended for use as a separate flat. This area created alongside the new swimming pool could be rented out or used by family members.

On the street level, the new large garage space, with corner windows letting in good light and surprising views, could be used as an office for running a small home business in addition to housing cars.

Before plans

1. Driveway, with steps to basement level
2. Single garage
3. Store
4. WC with shower
5. Staff bedroom

Street Level

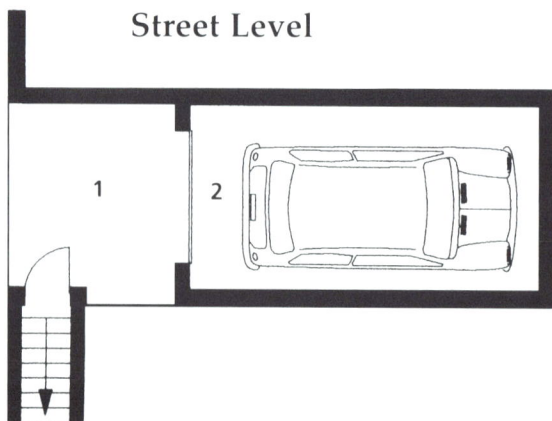

Basement Level

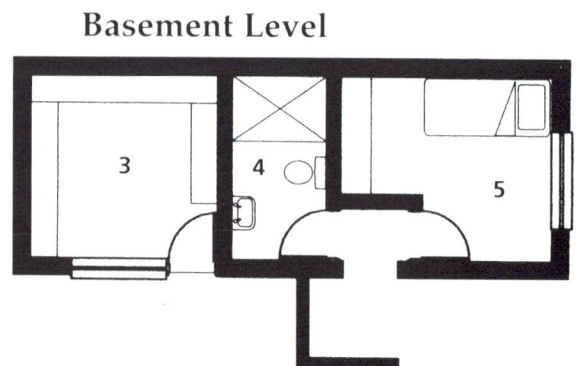

0m 1m 2m 3m 4m 5m

After plans

1. Entrance gate, with steps to basement level
2. Four-car garage/workshop
3. Living space
4. Shower room with WC
5. Kitchen

Street Level

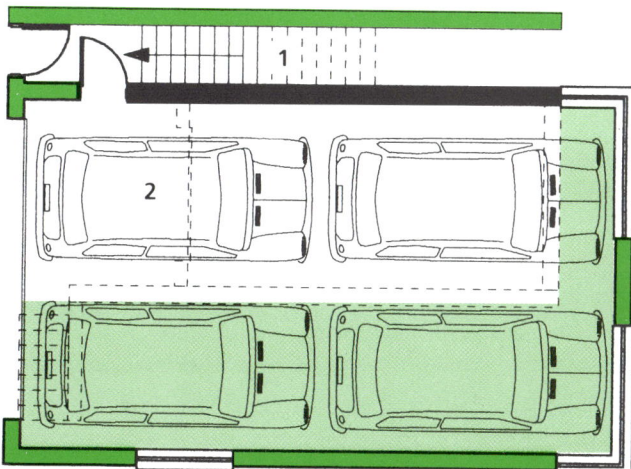

Basement Level

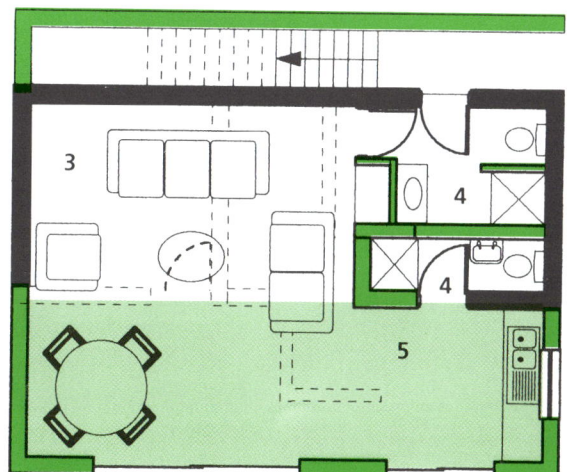

A separate outbuilding containing a single garage and storeroom was converted into a small living unit with a bedroom, bathroom and an open-plan kitchenette/living space. A door was added between the two existing spaces and a double-glazed entrance door links this space to a garden. The original garage door was removed and the opening bricked up so that the new living space did not overlook the main house driveway. In this way, the new living space is separate and private from the main house.

Before starting to plan this conversion, we asked the owners to check their property title deeds to see whether there were any restrictions related to changing the use of the outbuilding.

Before plan

1. Store
2. Garage

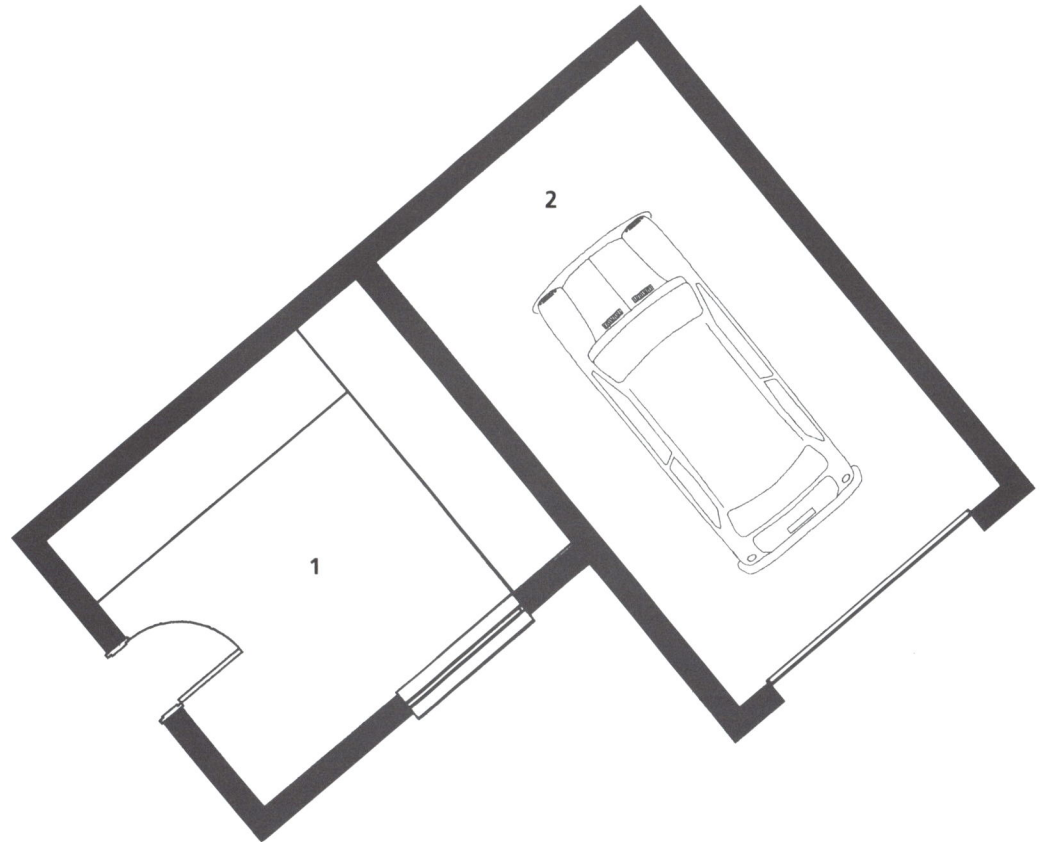

E S
North W

0m   1m   2m   3m   4m   5m

After plan

1a. Living/dining area, with
    bay window and double
    entrance doors
1b. Kitchenette
2a. Bathroom
2b. Bedroom

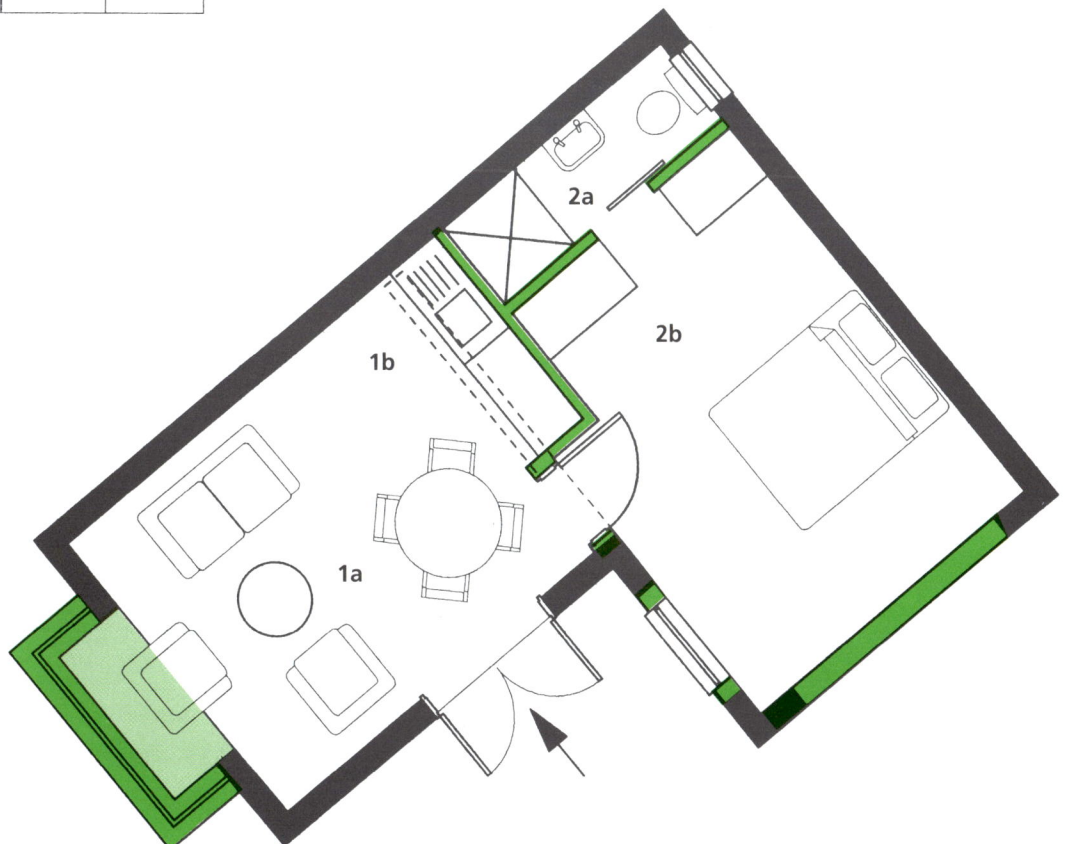

An untidy and disused outside store was linked to the main house, and the original kitchen was redesigned so that it combined with the extension to create an open-plan kitchen/playroom with a pergola patio to the side garden. This created a lovely east-facing outdoor breakfast patio.

The original kitchen door was moved so that it lined up with the front door. A glazed door was used between the kitchen and the entrance hall which now gives more light to the entrance hall and allows a view through the entrance hall to the rooflight-lit kitchen and playroom and to the garden. The lost store space was retrieved by adding built-in cupboards along one wall of the new playroom.

The extension was achieved using a simple lean-to roof structure which fitted neatly below and did not disturb the original main house roof. There was sufficient height in the rooms to allow for this. The original store walls were not suitable for re-use as they were damp and falling apart, but the original footings to these walls were used along with the doors and windows.

Before plan

1. Dining room
2. Entrance hall
3. Bedroom
4. Bedroom
5. Bedroom
6. Bathroom
7. Kitchen
8. Living room
9. Study
10. Store
11. WC outside

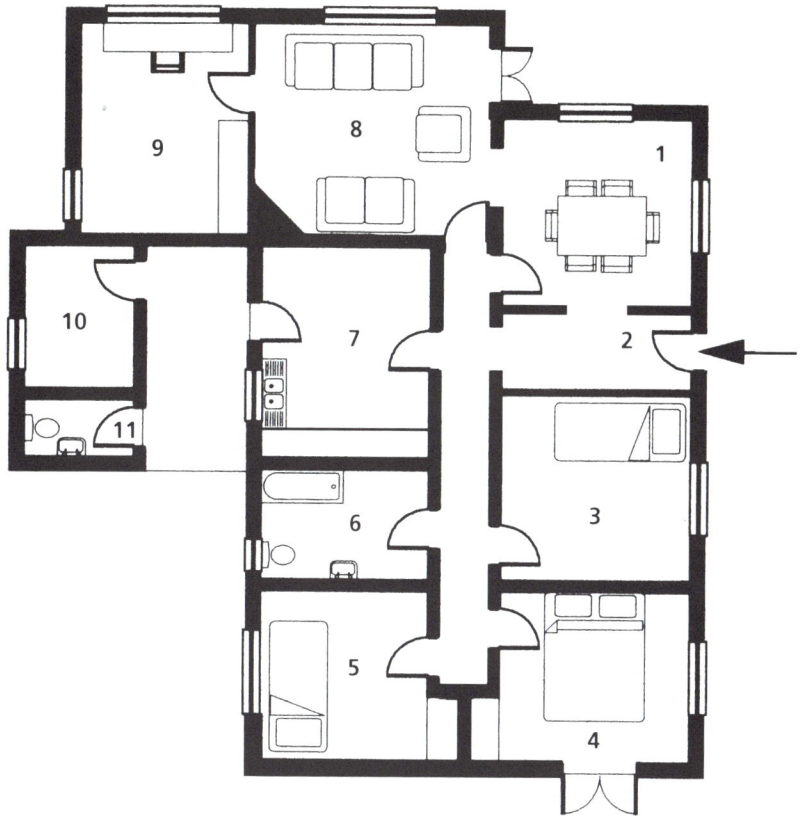

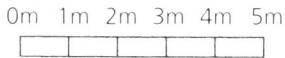

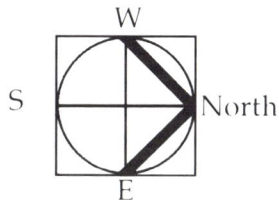

0m 1m 2m 3m 4m 5m

W
S   North
E

After plan

1. Dining room
2. Entrance hall
3. Bedroom
4a. Main bedroom, with new bay window
4b. En-suite WC with shower
5. Bedroom
6. Bathroom
7. New kitchen, with skylight
8. Living room
9. Study
10. Playroom (open plan to kitchen)
11. Patio and pergola, with built-in seat
12. New carport and covered walkway
    to back door

61

ADDING NEW SPACE

*Additions can range in scale from bay windows and porches to new rooms
and adding a new storey.*

Where you can add and how much you can add to the existing building is governed by:

- building regulations;
- cost;
- appearance; and
- the location of your home in relation to the site boundaries.

The most important consideration is integrating the addition with the existing house form and structure. Creating new space can:

- expand your house horizontally;
- link your house with an existing garage; or
- add a new storey to your single-storey home.

When adding to your home, you may find a solution that solves several problems and offers bonuses other than the creation of more space. This could include creating a useful outdoor area, gaining views, accessing a garden, improving the appearance of your home, improving circulation and flow, and bringing light to dark spaces.

EXTENSIONS AT THE BACK

The back of a home is normally a private space. Swimming pools are usually located in the back garden and this is more often than not the area where one finds laundries, washing lines and backyards. It is often a forgotten space, windswept and a place to let dogs run. These back spaces are very valuable and an extension can open up many uses which you may not have considered.

Disused outbuildings can be linked to the house or demolished to allow for more suitable extensions.

Hidden views can be opened up to the house, and garden space can be made more accessible and usable. If you can achieve a view through your home, from the front door to the back garden, this can make it feel bigger and more secure, and promotes a sense of unity with the surrounding spaces.

ADDITIONS AT THE SIDE

Often there is insufficient space on each side of your home to consider large extensions. Those extensions that do occur on the side of a home are usually a bathroom or stores. Side extensions will depend on the size of the property.

Check the town planning regulations for your area as nowadays it is acceptable practice to build up to the side boundaries (taking your neighbours into consideration). When considering additions to the side of your home remember:

- *to maintain access paths* all the way around your home or at least down one side, allowing for flow from the back to the front of your property without having to walk through your home (for example, for garden services, swimming pool services or carrying refuse bags to the street). Alternatively, to improve the security of the property you may consider closing off one of the sides from front to back.
- *the proportion of your home.* For example, does the extension make an already long, rectangular home appear stretched or uncomfortable on the site?

ADDITIONS AT THE FRONT

These are the most important extensions from an aesthetic point of view as they may change the appearance of your home dramatically. For this reason, they need to be carefully and sensitively considered. Take particular note of the front building line on your property as the town planning regulations related to this setback are around 4,5 m from the street boundary.

The popular idea of building a garage on the street boundary for easy access and security often results in problems with the local authorities in terms of the conditions of your property title deeds and town planning regulations. You need to consider the impact of the extension not only on your home but on the neighbourhood and street. If it is well designed and well built, a front extension can enhance and upgrade the character of the street and prompt your neighbours to improve their own properties.

DOUBLE-STOREY ADDITIONS

Here too, the character of a home can be affected significantly, especially if the upper floor extension is at the front of the property. The most important consideration for a double-storey extension is the shape of the existing roof and how this will be affected by the extension. Try, if possible, to avoid internal guttering where the existing roof slopes towards a new raised wall extension as this could create a potential waterproofing hazard. It may be necessary to build a new roof over your entire home or lift the existing roof (re-using trusses and roof material) if the footprint of your home is not extended. Another option to limit the height of the double-storey extension is to raise the roof by about a metre and replan the roof's structural system so that the new rooms are partially within the roof space and the ceilings slope to the underside of the roof. You may need to consider adding dormer-type windows with this sort of extension.

LINKING TO OUTBUILDINGS

Outbuildings are often underused because of their lack of accessibility. They could be converted into guest suites or incorporated into your home, giving you valuable added space at not too much additional cost. Check the structure of the outbuilding, as often, due to neglect, it may not be feasible to consider using these spaces. It may be necessary to demolish the walls and only use the existing foundations (in extreme cases), but, on the whole, unused stores and obsolete staff quarters or stables can be successfully incorporated into your home.

This small cottage was turned into a family home with three bedrooms, two bathrooms, a study, a double garage and a swimming pool. In this example, the existing historical cottage was sensitively renovated to keep its original character.

The original single garage located at the back of the property was converted into a main bedroom with an en-suite bathroom. Glazed doors were added, giving access to a garden. A flat-roofed link connects the converted garage to the cottage. A new entrance courtyard and double garage were added and the original cottage was extended at the back with the addition of a patio and steps.

Within the cottage, the roof timbers of the living spaces were exposed and a rooflight was added, giving a mountain view, light and a feeling of space.

The existing bathroom was upgraded and an outside shower added to the kitchen yard area. Open-plan kitchen fittings were included in the dining space which leads off the new patio to the long back garden.

The once dark cottage is now light. It feels spacious yet cosy and offers good flow from the house to the outside spaces at the front and back of the property. Cars can be securely parked off the street and the double garage serves as a children's playroom off the entrance courtyard.

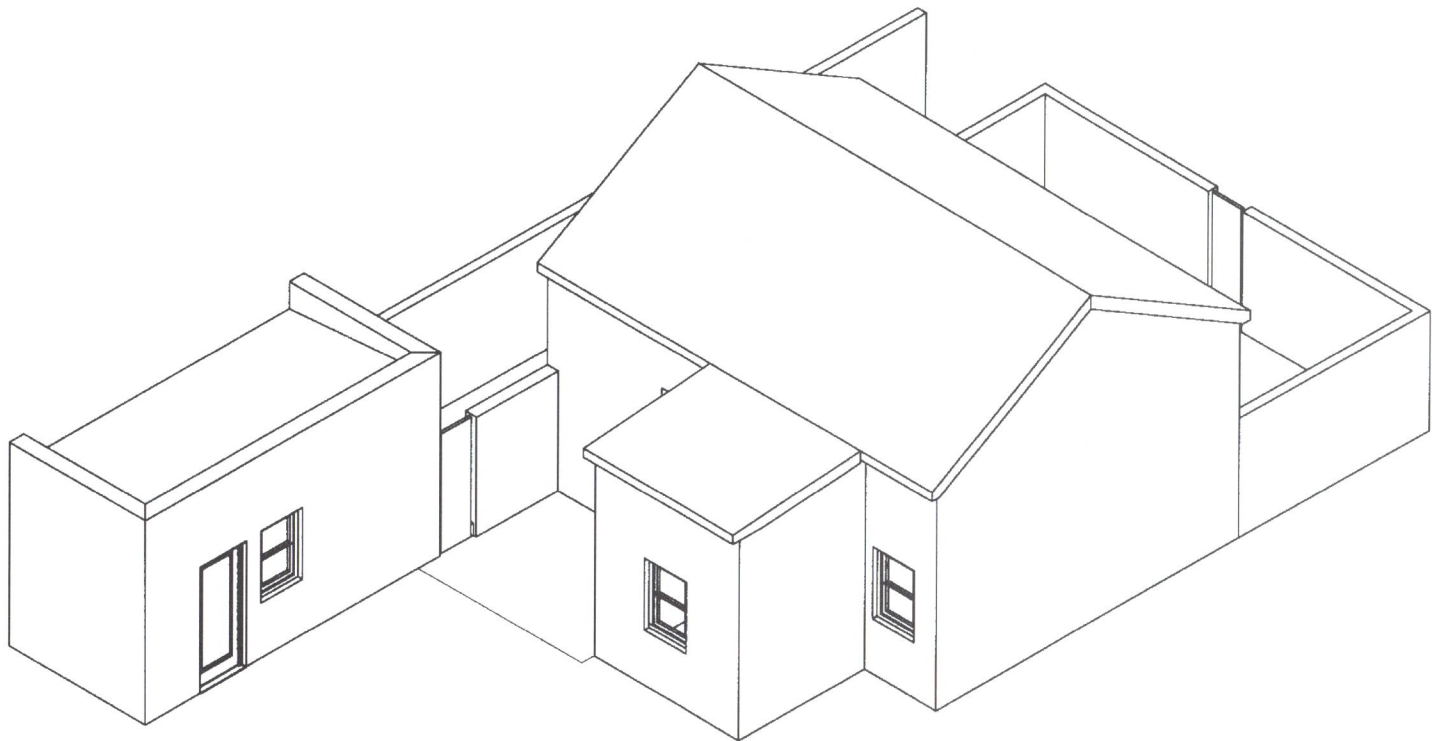

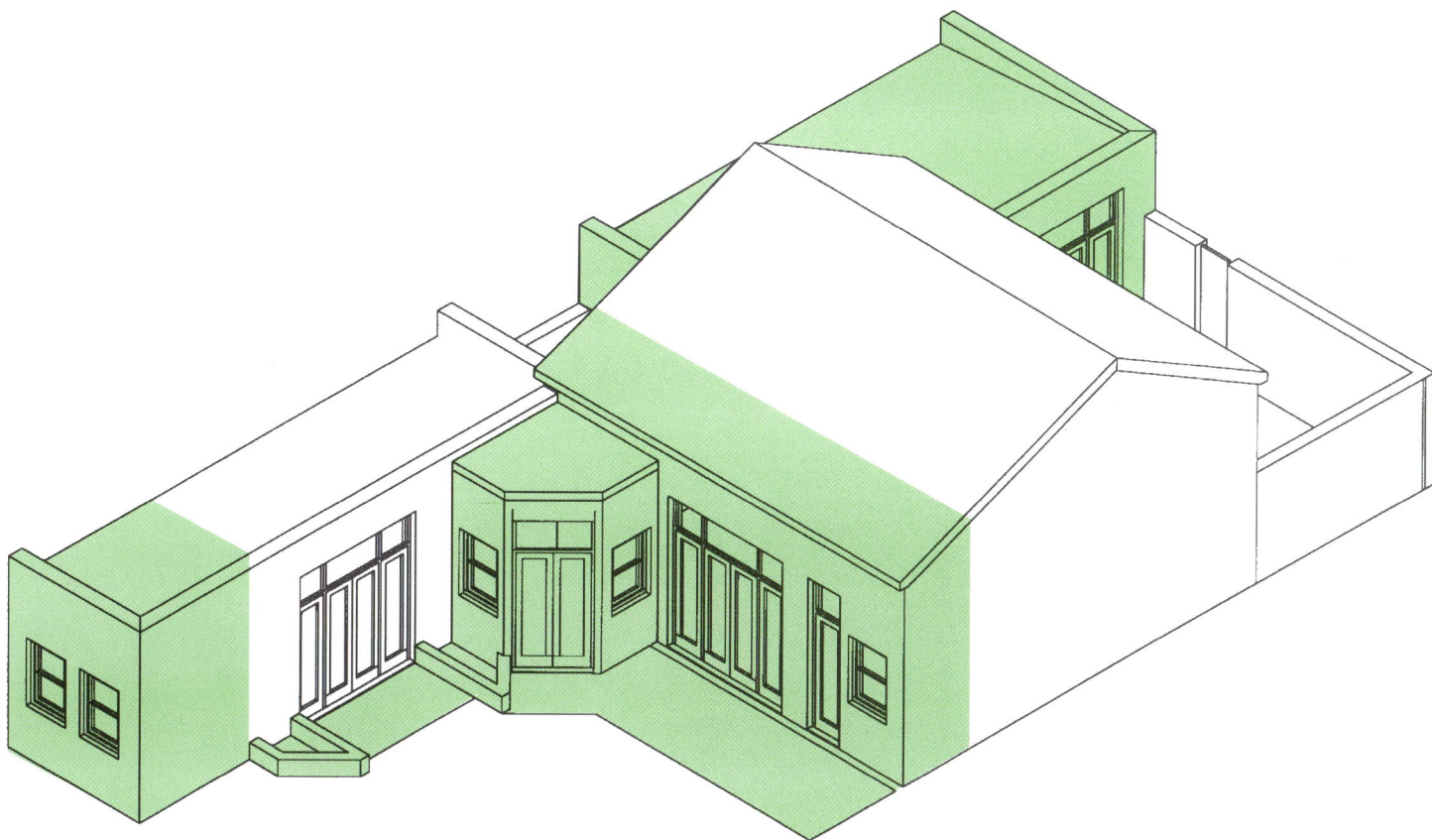

Before plan

1. Garage
2. Driveway
3. Courtyard
4. Kitchen
5. Bedroom
6. Dining room
7. Living room
8. Bathroom
9. Bedroom
10. Entrance courtyard

0m   1m   2m   3m   4m   5m

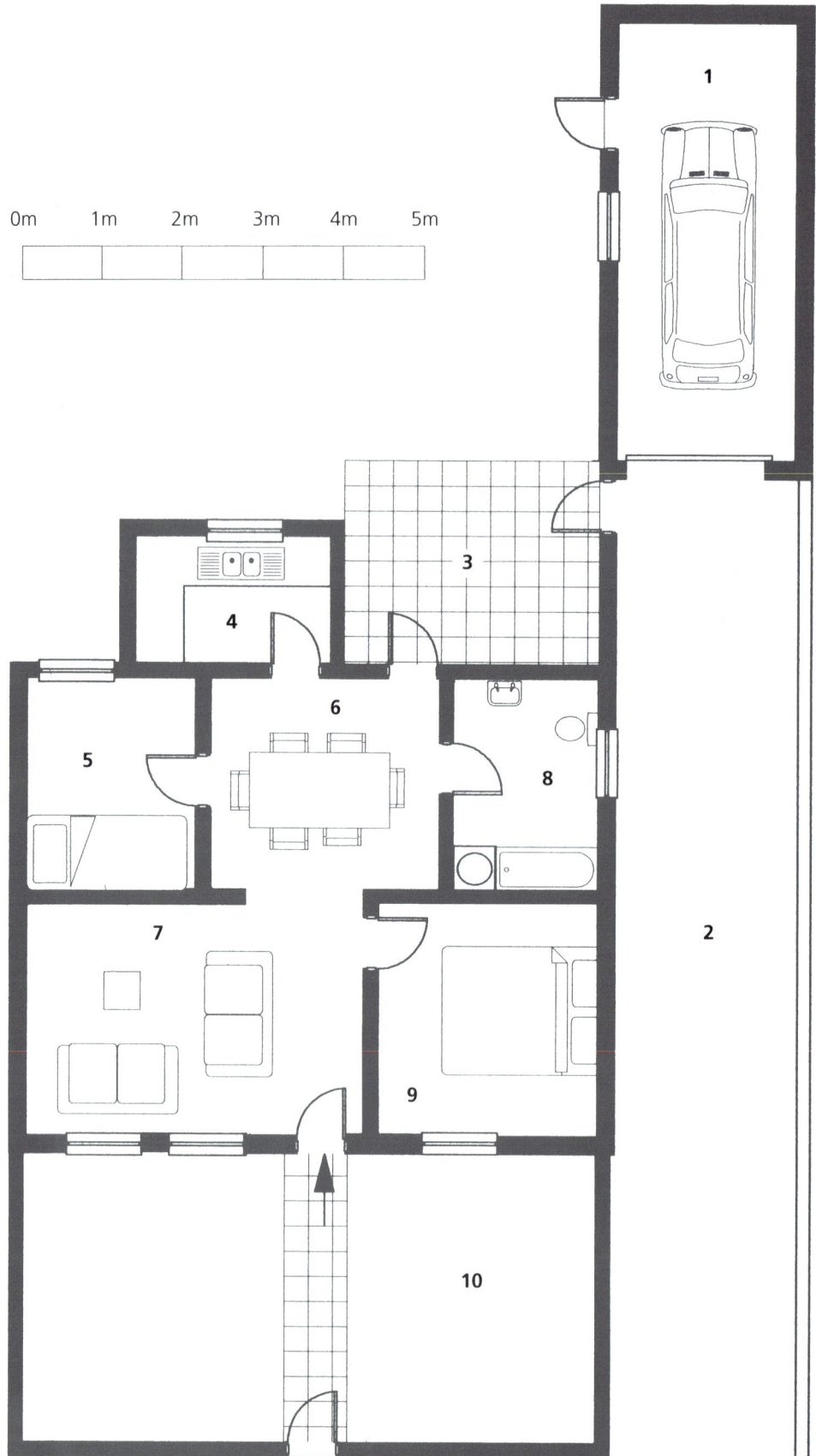

1

3

4

6

5

8

7

2

9

10

After plan

1. Main bedroom (converted garage), with en-suite bathroom and doors to garden
2. Planters
3. Laundry
4. Kitchen
5. Bedroom
6. Dining room
7. Lounge
8. Bathroom
9. Study
10. Entrance courtyard
11. Courtyard
12. Bedroom
13. Double garage
14. Swimming pool

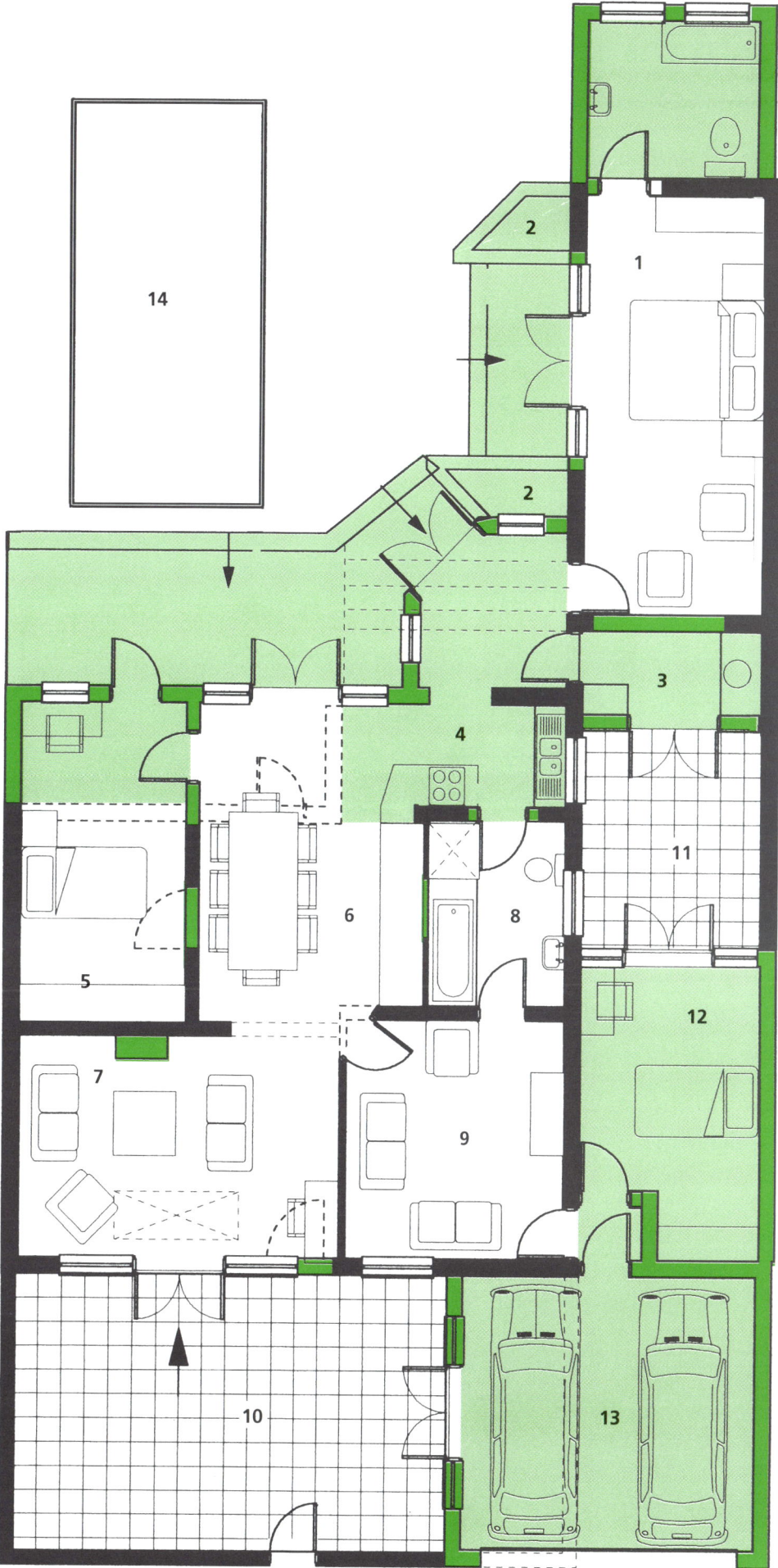

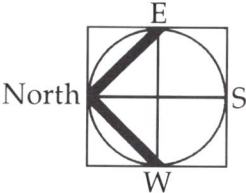

This house is located on a sloping site and the front of the house is much higher than the back. The existing entrance balcony was enclosed to create a new entrance hall. A double garage was created, which offers access from the main house to a tiled patio (across the garage roof). The original single garage has been converted into a garden-level playroom for children which leads directly to the new garage and to the garden. The glass-enclosed spiral stair added to the main house creates secure undercover access from the lower-level garage to the upper-level home.

Internally, the main house was subject to minor alterations to create an open-plan kitchen to the living spaces, and the kitchen and bathroom spaces were interchanged. The kitchen is now closest to the new spiral stair access and the bathroom is central. An existing bathroom was made into an en-suite for the main bedroom by simply changing the location of the door and the washbasin.

Before street-level plan

1. Unusable space under house
2. Garage
3. Store

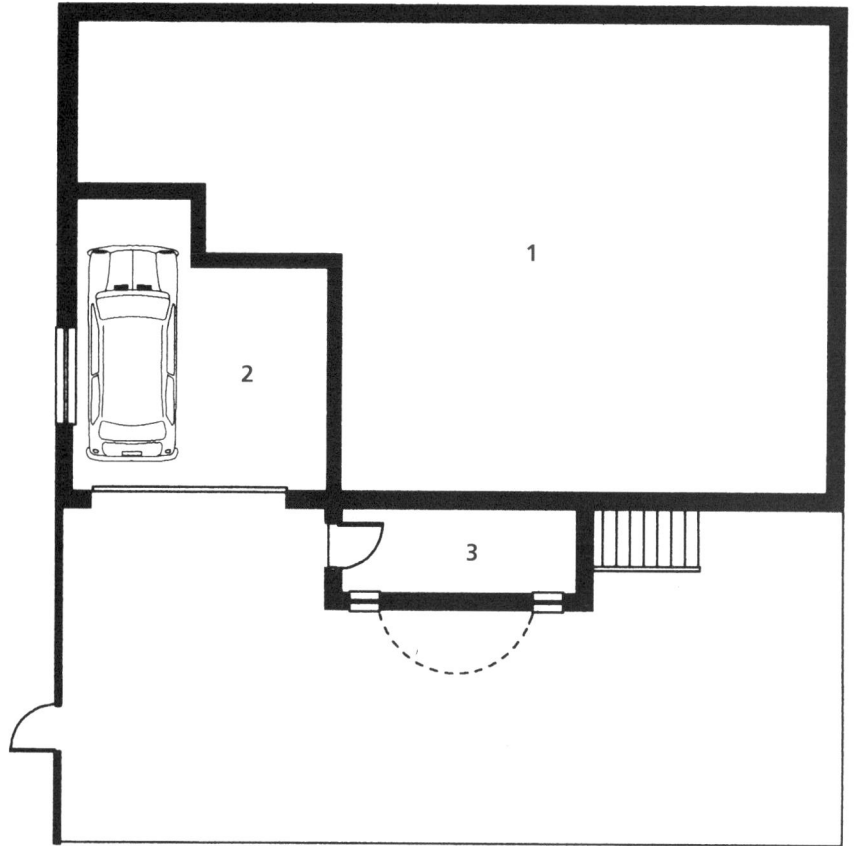

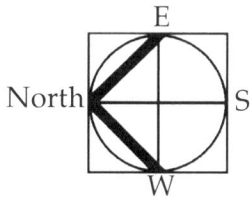

E
North — S
W

Before upper-level plan

1. Bathroom
2. Kitchen
3. Bedroom
4. Bedroom, with en-suite bathroom
5. Living/dining room
6. Main bedroom
7. Front porch

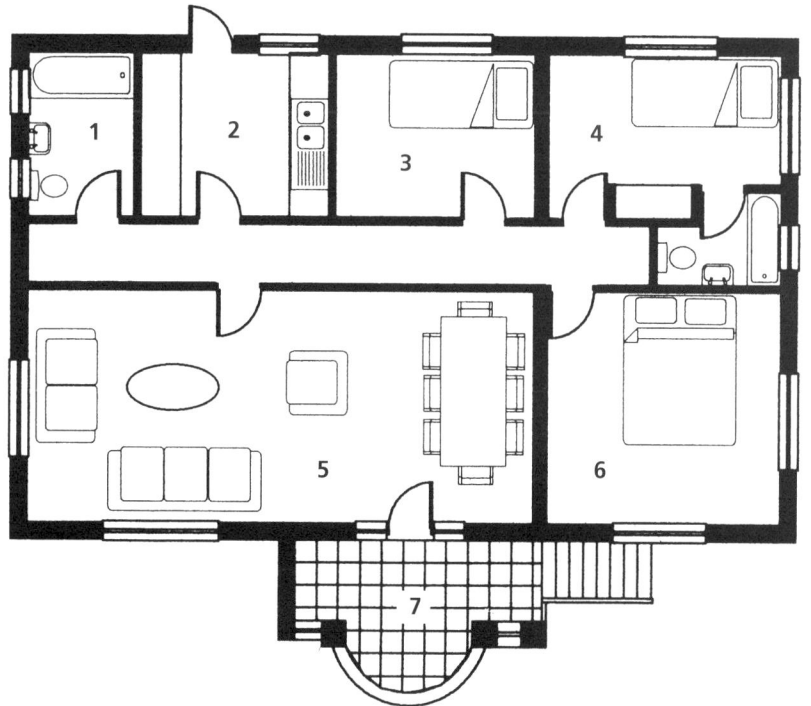

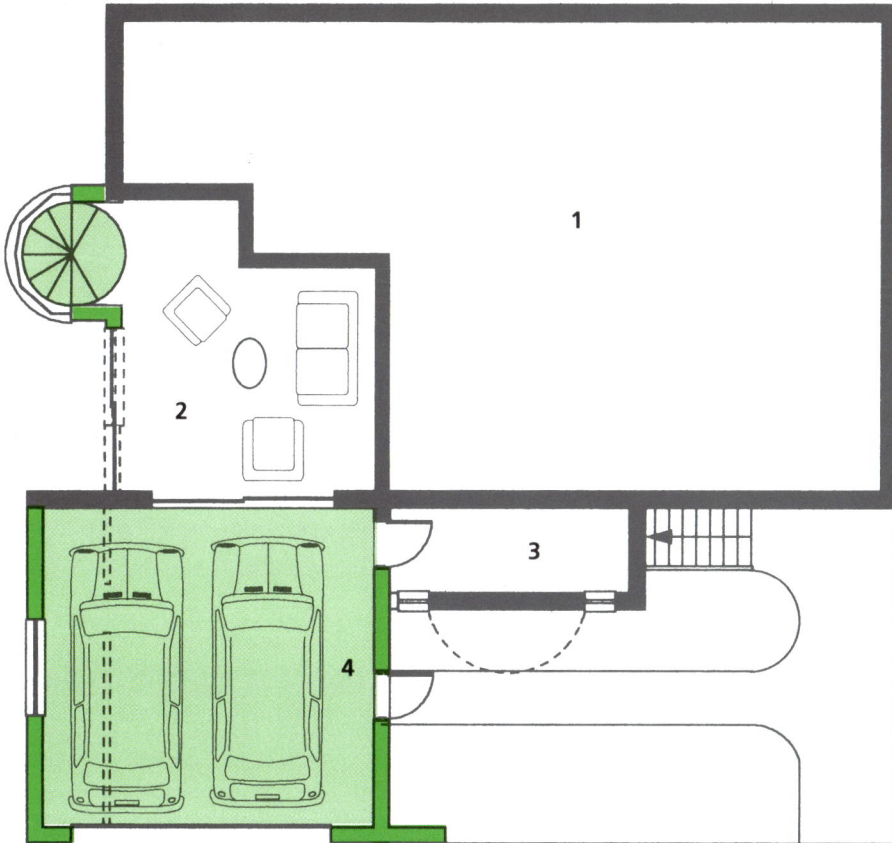

After street-level plan

1. Unusable space under house
2. New playroom, with sliding doors to garden and spiral staircase to house, giving undercover access from garage
3. Store
4. Double garage

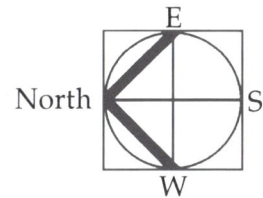

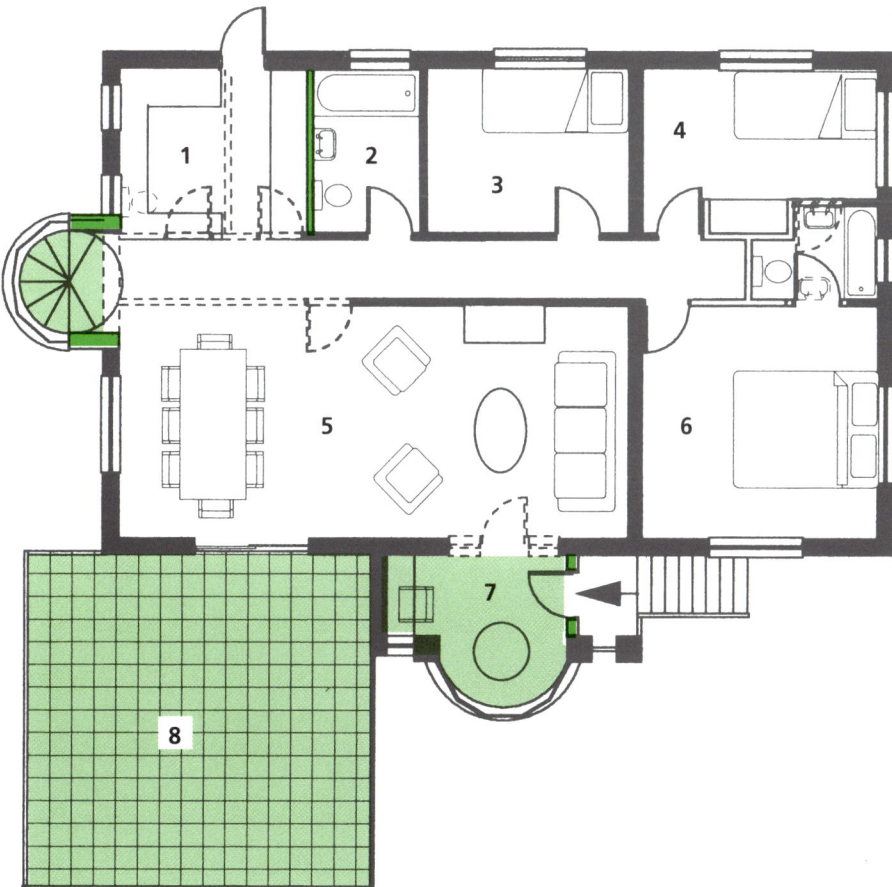

After upper-level plan

1. Open-plan kitchen
2. Bathroom
3. Bedroom
4. Bedroom
5. Living/dining room, with spiral staircase to playroom, and sliding doors to patio over garage
6. Main bedroom, with en-suite bathroom
7. Entrance hall (enclosed balcony)
8. Patio over new garage

0m 1m 2m 3m 4m 5m

PLAN 18

Dilapidated sheds and stores were demolished to allow for this extension towards the back of the home and to open up the house to a large unused back garden which faces west, with sun and views.

The small pokey kitchen and damp bathroom were demolished and moved to new locations: the bathroom, accessible from a central passage to the side of the house, and the kitchen made into an open-plan counter to one side of the new living room. A large fireplace was built in the living room and two bay windows were added, on the garden side, allowing for sitting space off the kitchen (for breakfast) and off the living space for a small dining table. The house assumed an aura of grandeur as small spaces were linked together to create a large, much needed living/entertaining area leading to a private back garden. The French doors to the garden were positioned in line with the original dark central passage, allowing for long views through the house from front to back and lighting the passage.

A glazed door was positioned between the passage and the new living space so that it could be closed to contain the heat from the fire in winter.

Before plan

1. Bedroom
2. Bedroom
3. Bedroom
4. Living room
5. Kitchen
6. Yard
7a. Shed
7b. Store
8. Garage
9. Outside WC

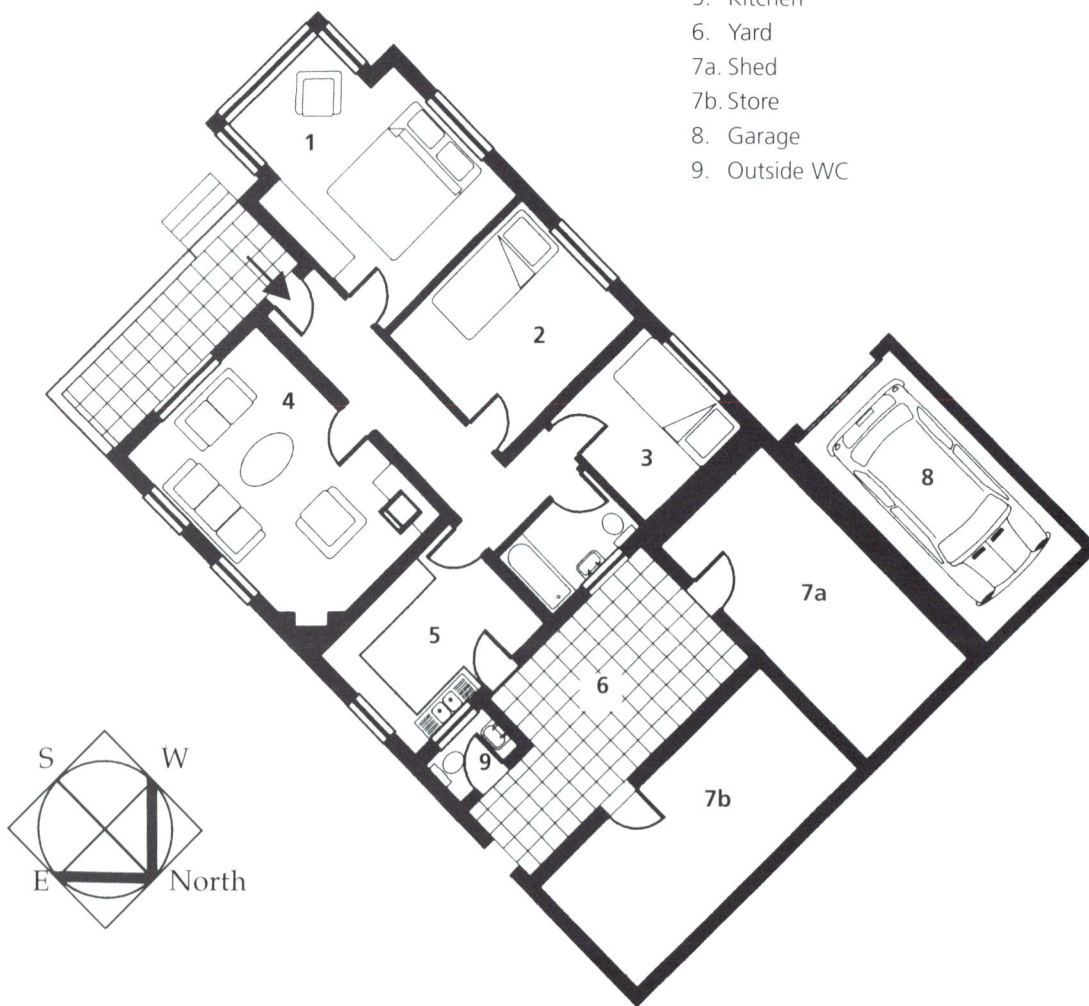

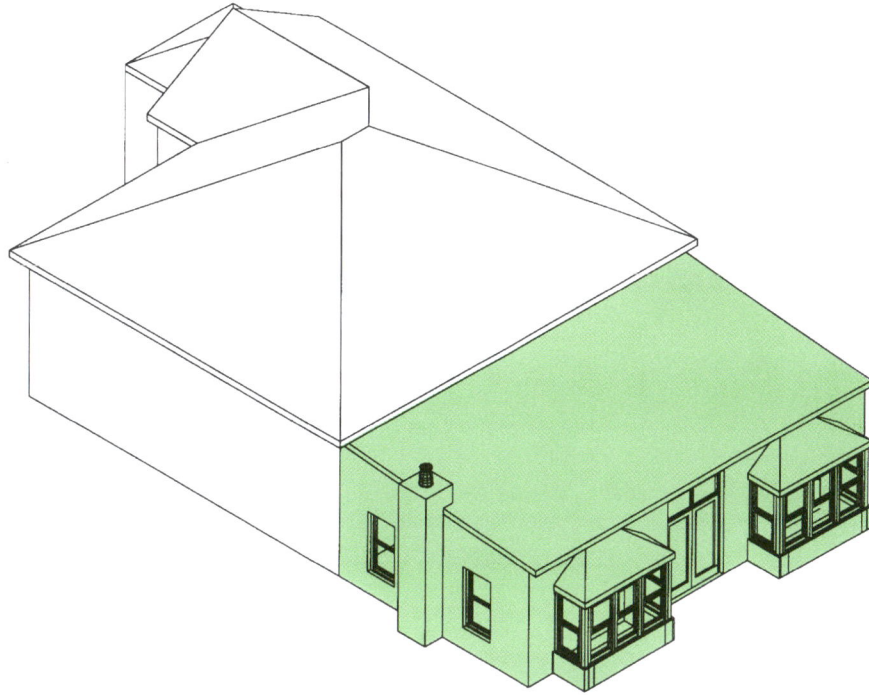

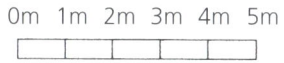

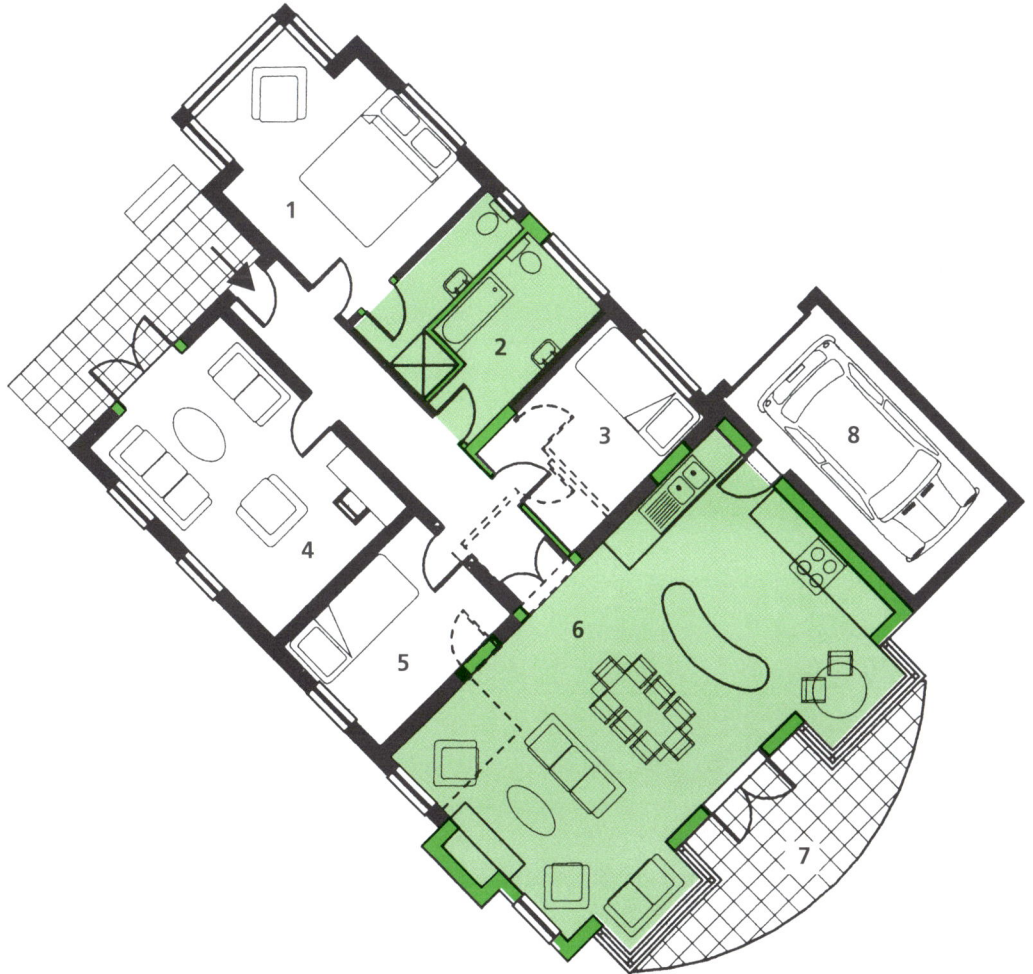

0m 1m 2m 3m 4m 5m

After plan

1. Main bedroom, with en-suite bathroom
2. Bathroom
3. Bedroom
4. Lounge with doors to front patio
5. Bedroom/study
6. Living/dining room/kitchen, with fireplace, bay window and doors to patio
7. Patio
8. Garage

A grand old home had its front aspect improved by better flow to the new raised garden. A pergola-covered patio leads directly off the living spaces and is partially covered to allow for comfortable access from a new double garage located at the lower street level of the property.

The problem of access from the street is solved through the addition of a secure double garage on the street boundary (there was precedent for this in the neighbourhood). Part of the original single garage is used as a workroom at the back of the new double garage. The new garage doors are operated by remote control. Stairs leading from the back of the garage/workshop give direct access to the covered patio above and to the main house. The original garden was raised considerably along with the front boundary wall which is designed as a retaining wall. The raised garden is now at the main house level allowing for easy flow directly from the house. A swimming pool was added in the new raised section of ground, which minimised the amount of soil required to raise the garden to the house level.

The original pedestrian access was enhanced and rebuilt as part of the new street boundary wall with a secure metal-railing gate with remote access from the house. The metal-rail theme is continued above the new street boundary wall which has piers and railings to make the most of the views from the property and to minimise the height of the new wall on the street side. The columns used for the new patio pergola match the style of the balcony columns on the front facade of the existing home.

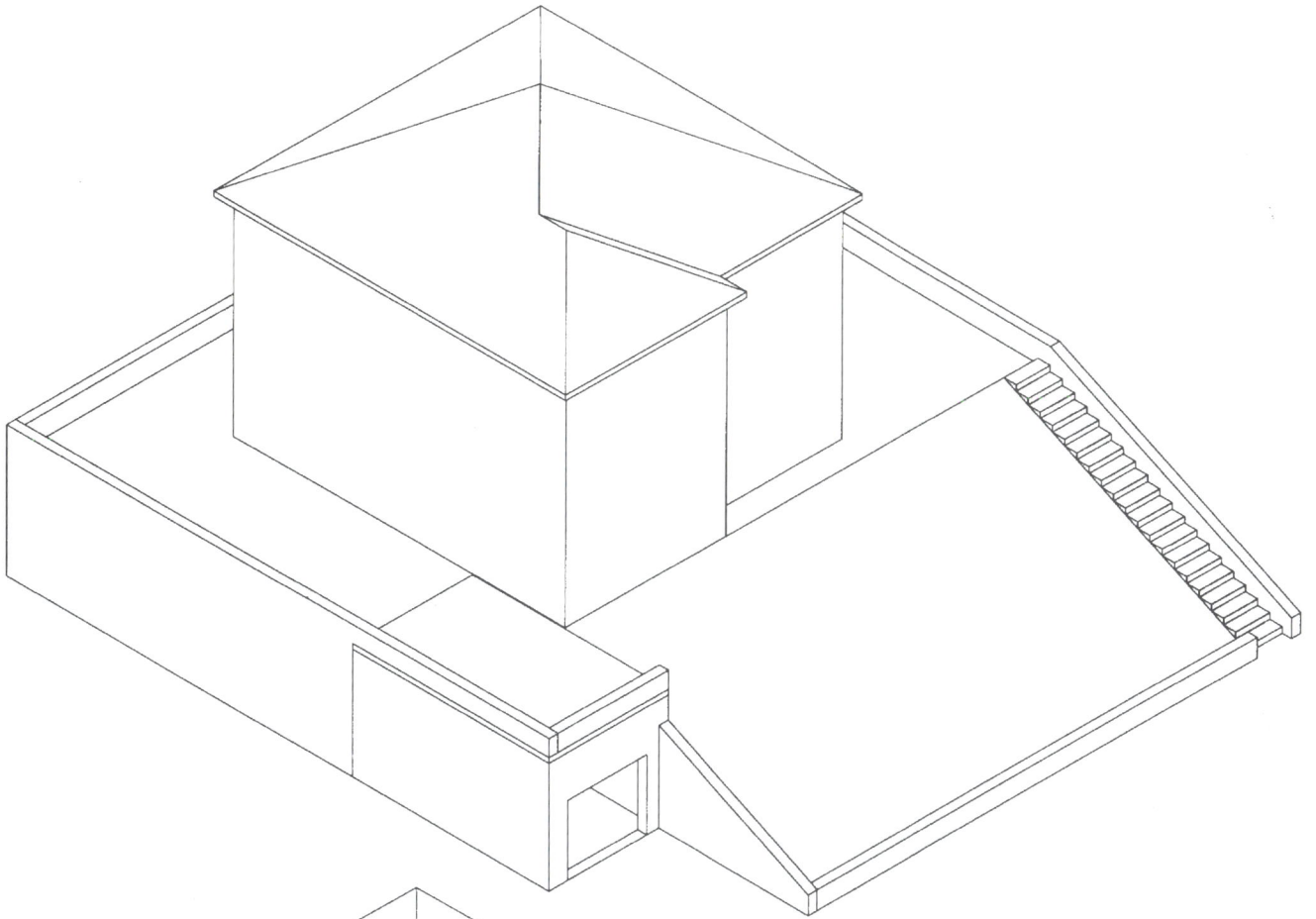

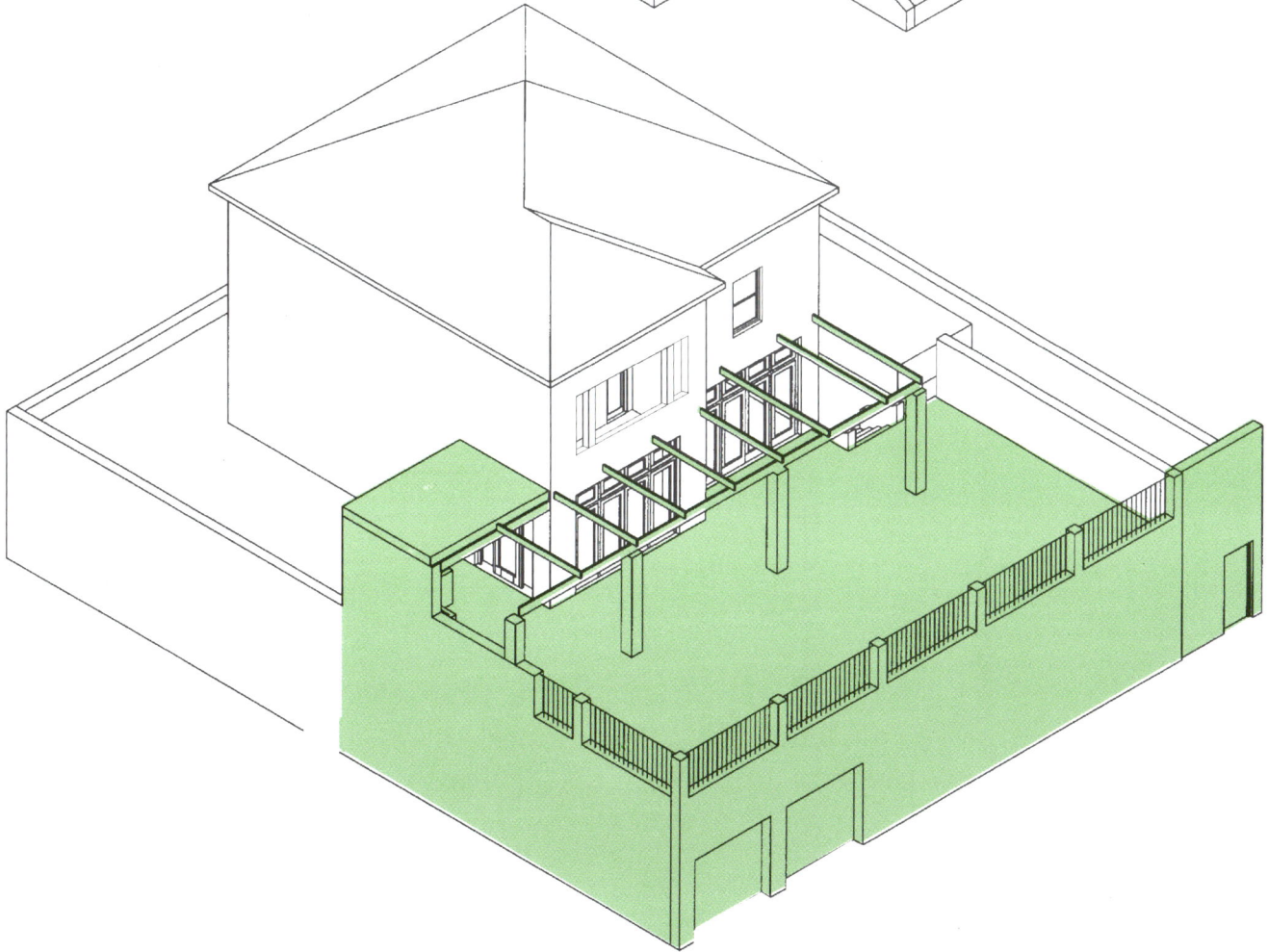

Before ground-level plan

1. Garage roof
2. Enclosed stoep
3. Steps from garden to garage roof
4. Sloped garden
5. Driveway at street level

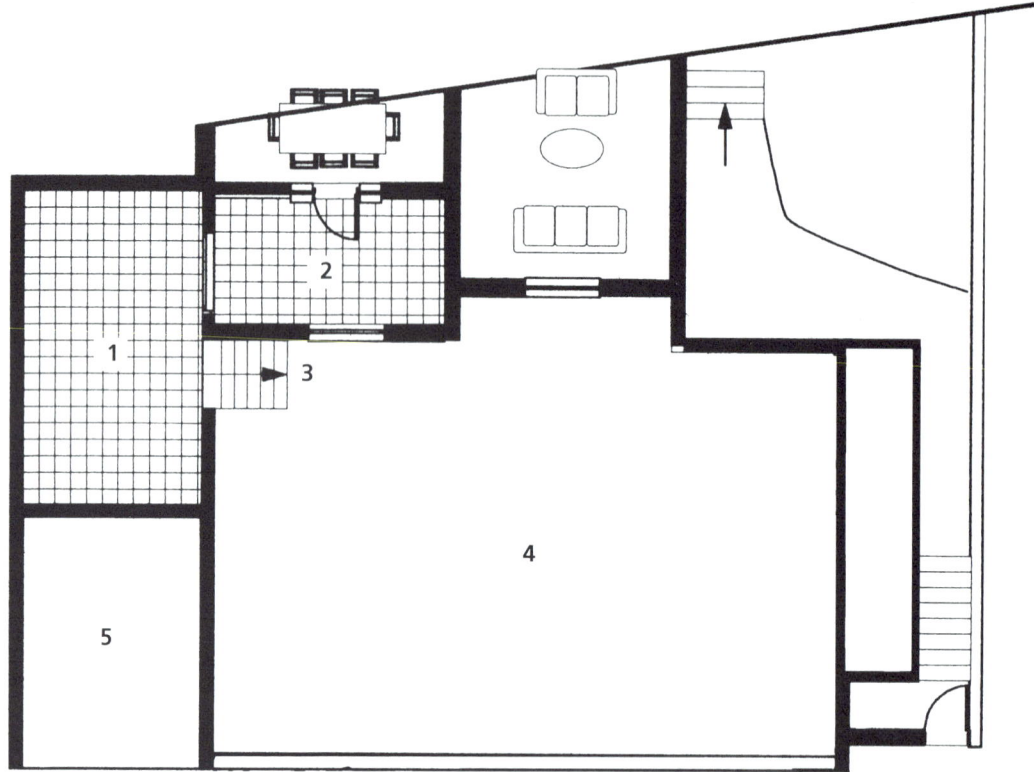

Before street-level plan

1. Garage
2. Driveway
3. Entrance to property

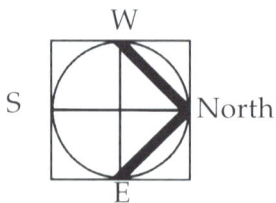

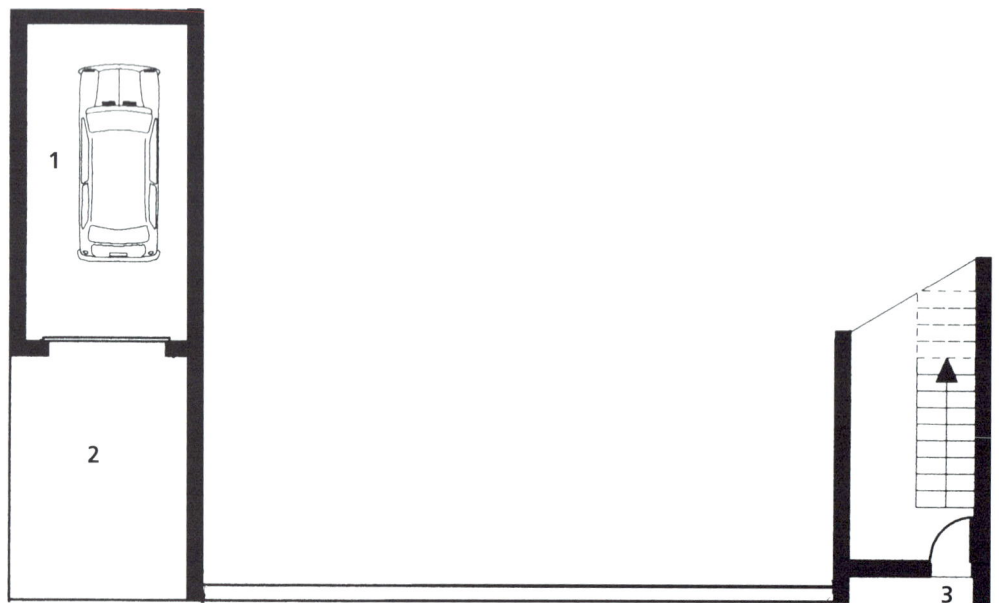

After ground-level plan

1. Steps to garage
2. Covered patio
3. Patio and pergola
4. Lawn above new garage
5. Swimming pool
6. Entrance to property

0m 1m 2m 3m 4m 5m

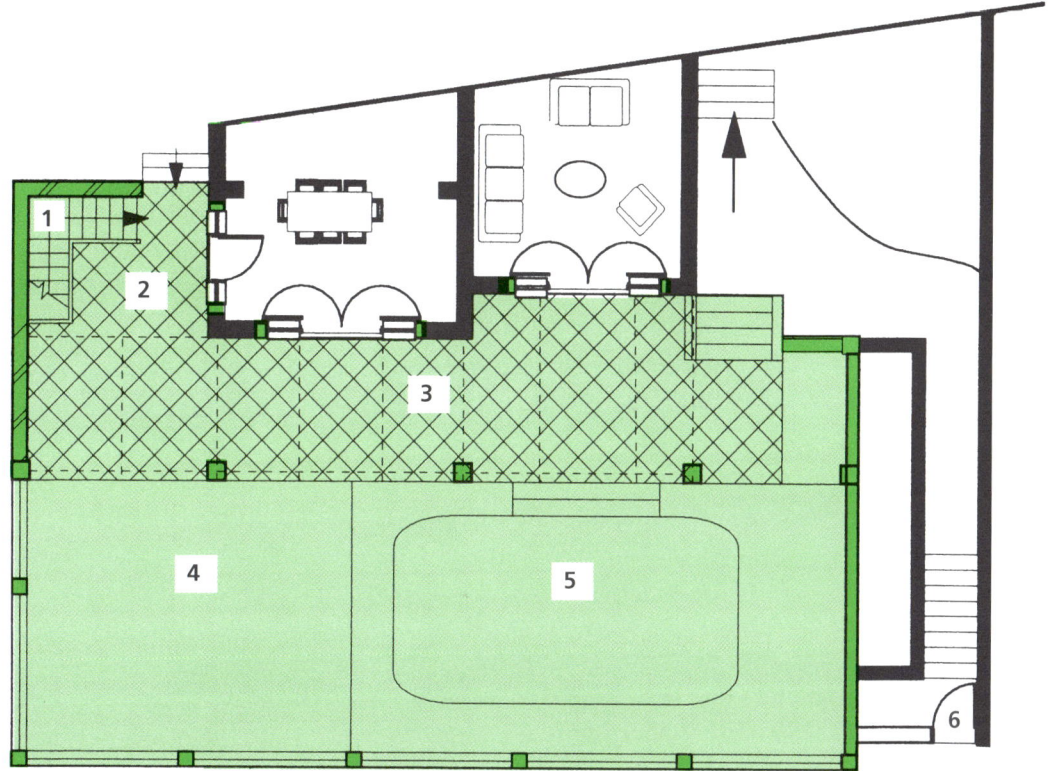

After street-level plan

1. Steps from garage
2. Double garage
3. Retaining walls
4. Front wall (replaces hedge)
5. Entrance to property

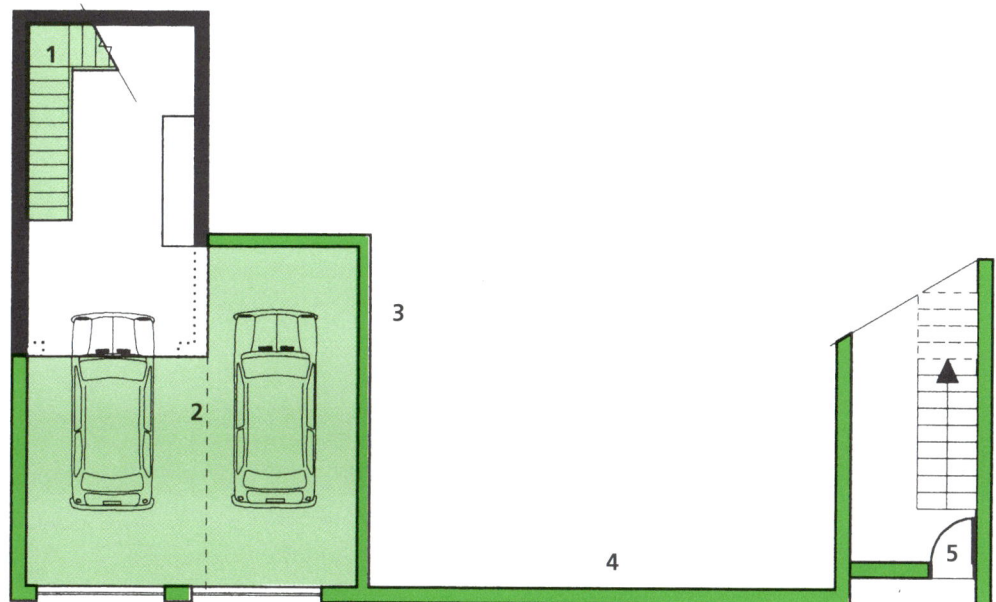

77

A new wing, comprising a study, a bathroom and a bedroom, was added to this Mediterranean-style house. The bathroom is located centrally, between the study and bedroom, giving easy access from both of these rooms.

The bedroom is located at the end of the extension, with its own private access to a side garden courtyard. A door was installed in the passage of this extension so that the bedroom and bathroom could be separated from the main house and serve as a guest suite or rentable accommodation. A feature of this extension is the glass bay window located in the new bedroom with sliding doors to the garden courtyard.

The study looks onto the existing garden and has a brick-paved patio space leading directly off it.

Low walls and railings were added around this extension to tie in with the appearance of the main house and to secure the property's entrance from the street.

The style of the new extension echoes that of the main house. The arch motif around the main entrance door is repeated in the street-facing facade of the extension. A semicircular-shaped plastered-brick planter was added to the street facade, in front of the recessed arch, to give it some depth and shadow.

The new roof is hipped into the existing roof and finished with matching tiles.

After plan

1. Bedroom
2. Shower room
3. Bedroom
4. Dining room
5. Living room
6. Kitchen
7. Study
8. Bathroom
9. Lobby
10. Bedroom
11. Planter
12. Patio

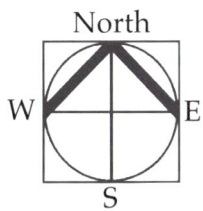

North

W   E

S

0m   1m   2m   3m   4m   5m

In this example, a double-storey extension was neatly added to the main house. The existing roof line was followed to create a harmonious link to the extension and this makes it appear as if it has always been part of the original house.

The brief for this extension was to add a bedroom area on an upper level to give access to views and to look over a north-facing garden. The existing ground-floor plan was also rearranged to create flow to the outside and to create a view through the house from the front door to the central courtyard. The original bathroom located in the centre of the house was moved to the side and the new large dining/living space leads onto a small light dining courtyard.

The existing garage at the side of the house was extended to form a double garage with direct undercover access to the new kitchen. A guest suite/staff quarters was added to the back of the garage space. The upper floor extension leads out onto a new deck which also acts as a cover for the new patio at ground-floor level.

Before plan

0m 1m 2m 3m 4m 5m

1. Garage
2. Staff quarters
3. Outside WC
4. Bedroom
5. Bedroom
6. Bathroom
7. Dining room
8. Verandah
9. Living room
10. Kitchen
11. Pantry
12. Yard

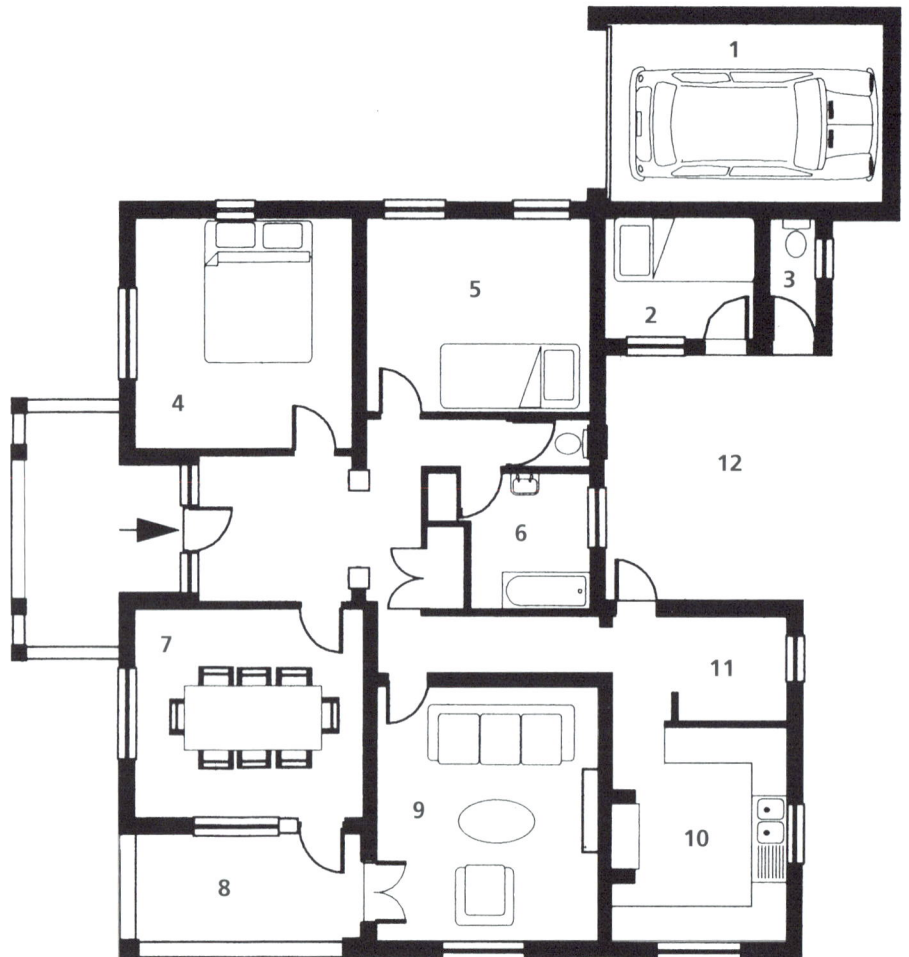

After upper-floor plan

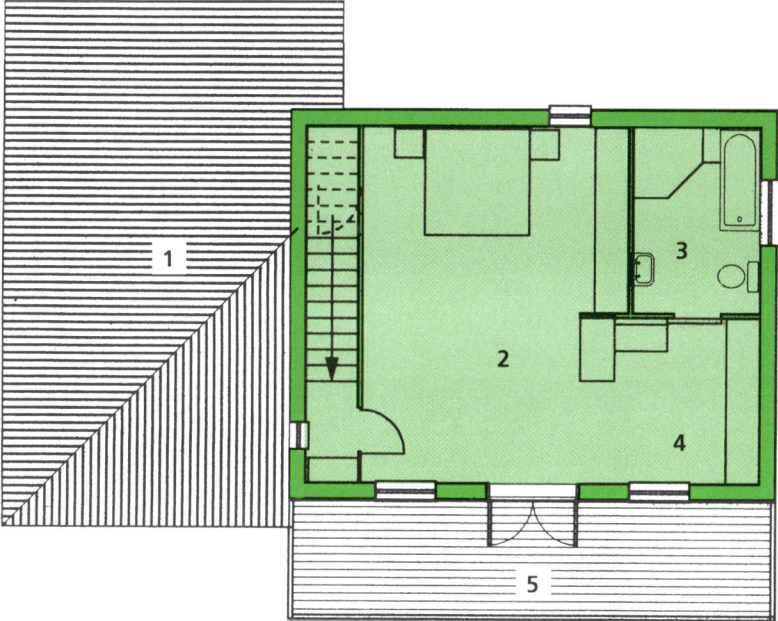

1. Part of original roof
2. Bedroom
3. Bathroom
4. Dressing room
5. Deck

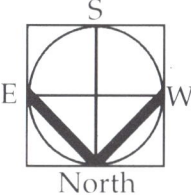

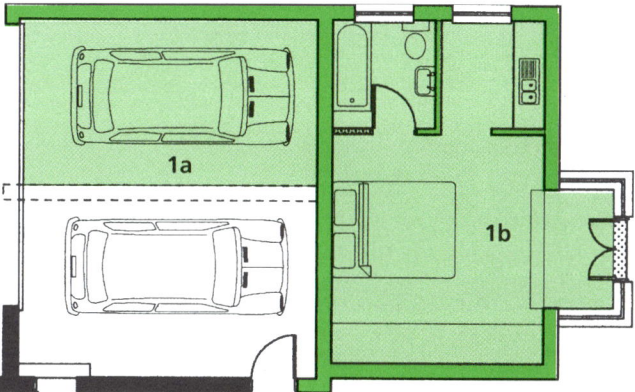

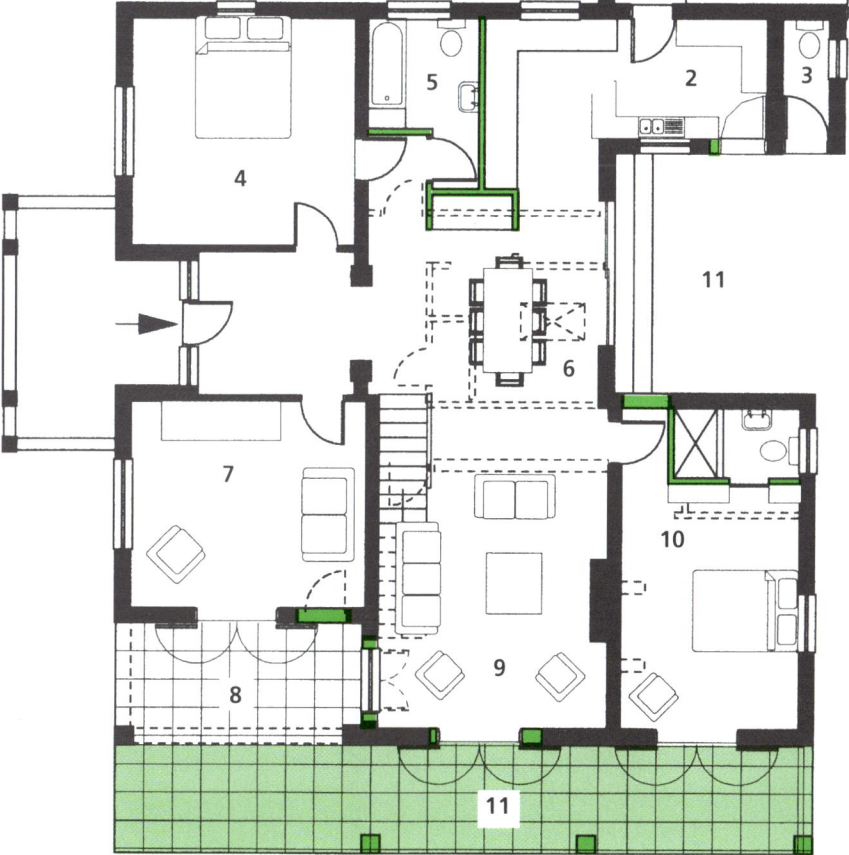

S

E W

North

After ground-floor plan

1a. Double garage
1b. Guest room, with en-suite bathroom
   and kitchenette
2. Kitchen
3. Outside WC
4. Bedroom
5. Bathroom
6. Dining room
7. TV room
8. Verandah
9. Living room
10. Bedroom, with en-suite bathroom
11. New patio

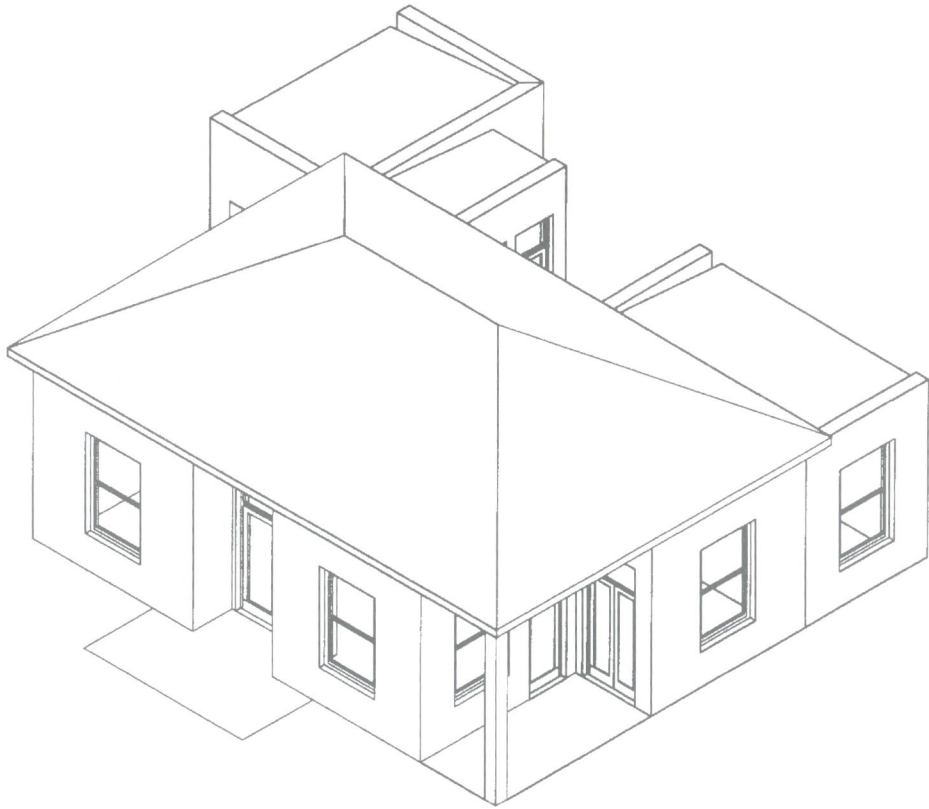

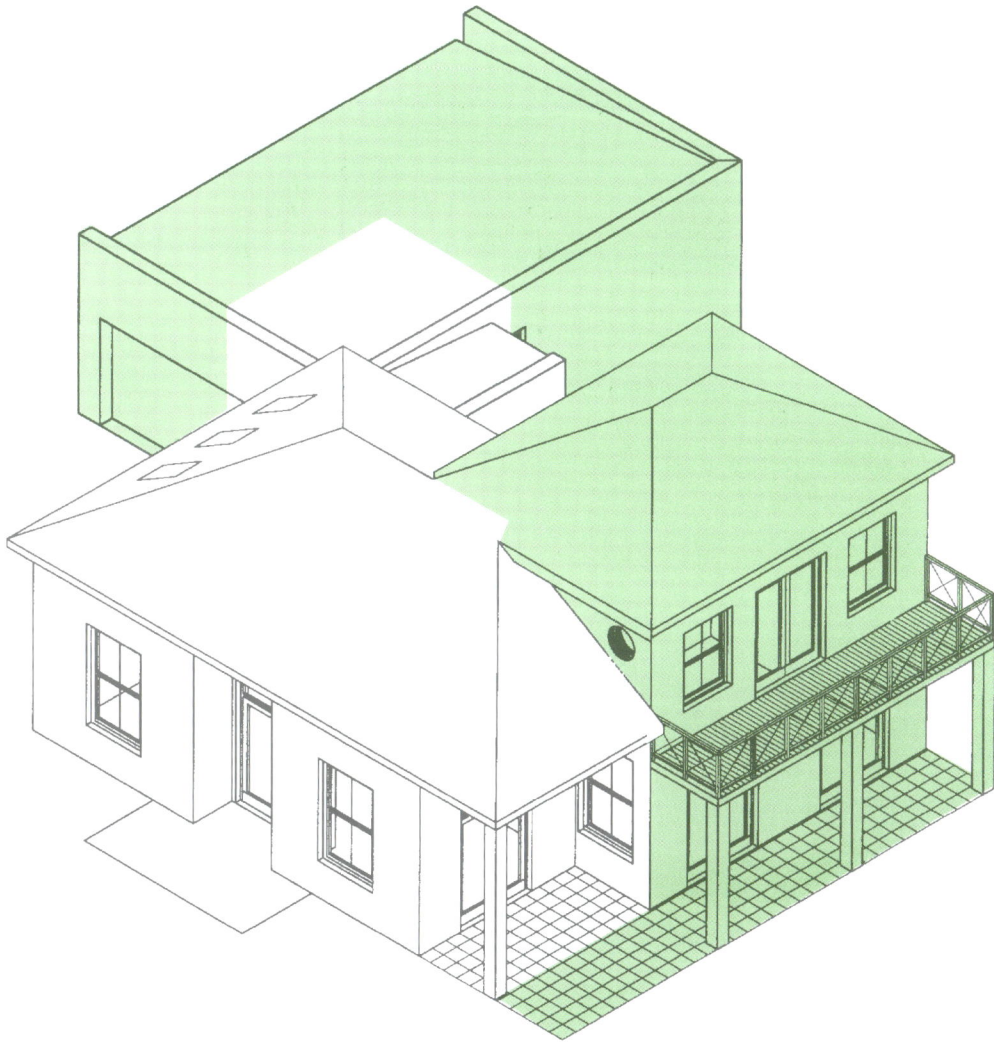

With a growing family, more bedrooms were needed in this small, two-bedroomed home located on a sloping site. The new back extension added two bedrooms and bathroom, and the house was re-planned according to an existing passage. This made for an easy extension, without having to reduce the size of the existing bedrooms or alter the existing home.

The sloping site meant that the new extension had to be raised above the main house level with some steps built inside the passage. To avoid the feel of a long passage to the new extension, French doors were included. These bring light to the space. A porch with a pergola for shade also leads off the bedrooms, creating an outdoor sitting space near the swimming pool and facing views. The bedrooms were located along the side boundary of the property with rooflights added for extra light as there is a well-established hedge between the property and neighbours which has been maintained for privacy and as a sound break.

The new extension was built in the same style as the original house with a front parapet wall, a plaster moulded band, and plastered and painted walls.

The French doors which link the two sections echo the style of the main house. The extension has opened up the use of the back garden space which is sunny and has previously unseen views. Locating the extension along the side of the house has meant that a large portion of the garden has been retained.

After plan

1. Living room
2. Dining room
3. Kitchen
4. Bedroom
5. Bedroom
6. Bathroom
7. Bathroom
8. Yard
9. Courtyard
10. Bedroom
11. Bathroom
12. Bedroom
13. Patio
14. Swimming pool

Existing

New

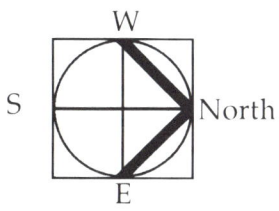

PLAN 23

A separate guest suite was added to this double-storey home. The original outbuilding/stores were demolished to make way for this suite which includes a bedroom with a north-facing bay window, and a new bathroom with shower, washbasin and toilet. The covered link from the main house to the guest suite and to the garden and kitchen yard was maintained, and the guest suite could be rented out with its own separate entrance.

A glazed double door replaced a window in the dining room, and now gives direct access from this room to the garden. The door also allows for an easier flow from the kitchen to the garden when the family are eating outside or entertaining guests.

Before plan

1. Bedroom
2. Bedroom
3. Kitchen
4. Yard
5. Store
6. Living room
7. Dining room
8. Playroom

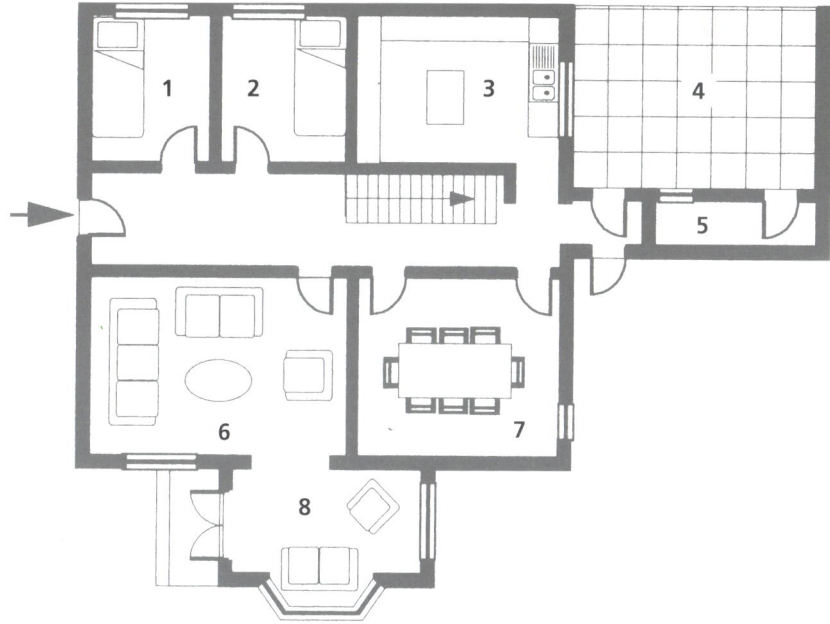

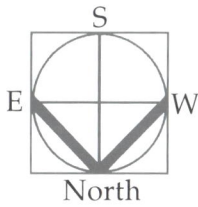

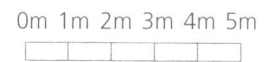

S
E W
North

0m 1m 2m 3m 4m 5m

After plan

1. Bedroom
2. Bedroom
3. Kitchen
4. Yard
5a. Bedroom, with new bay window
5b. Bathroom
6. Living room
7. Dining room
8. Playroom

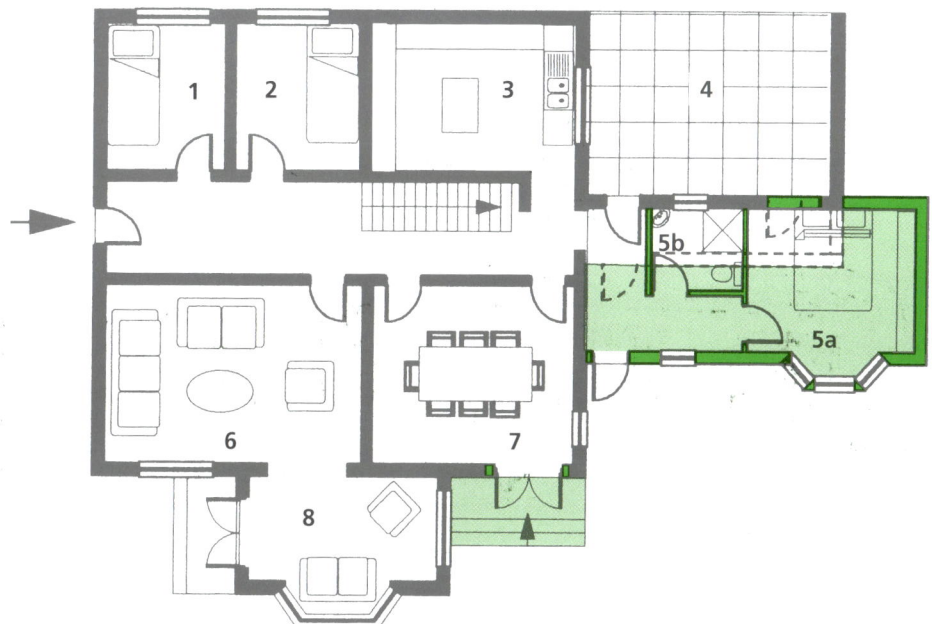

This Spanish-style home was extended forward with the addition of a new double garage. The living space increased and a new entrance hall was created. The original single garage was converted into a children's playroom.

The new double garage offers secure access from the street to the house through a door leading directly from the new garage into the converted single garage.

A feeling of space and light is achieved in the new dining area by exposing the roof timbers and painting them white, adding a sloped ceiling between the timbers, and installing opening rooflights for natural ventilation.

A glass-block screen cuts off the view from the front door to the bedroom passage without obscuring light from the new dining space.

Double French-type doors were added to the back of the converted garage/playroom allowing access for the children directly to the outside space at the side of the house.

The style of the original home was maintained in the new extension.

Before plan

1. Bathroom
2. Bedroom
3. Study
4. Outside WC
5. Bathroom
6. Bedroom
7. Bedroom
8. Kitchen
9. Dining room
10. Living room
11. Garage

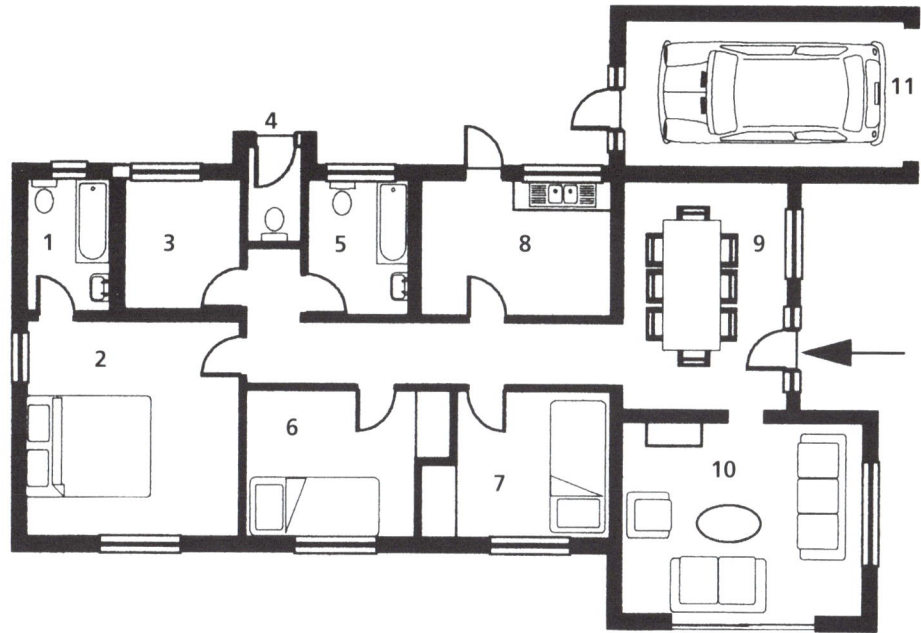

After plan

1. Bathroom
2. Bedroom
3. Study
4. Outside WC
5. Bathroom
6. Bedroom
7. Bedroom
8. Kitchen
9. Extended dining area, with skylight
10. Living area extended
11. Playroom (converted garage)
12. New double garage

0m 1m 2m 3m 4m 5m

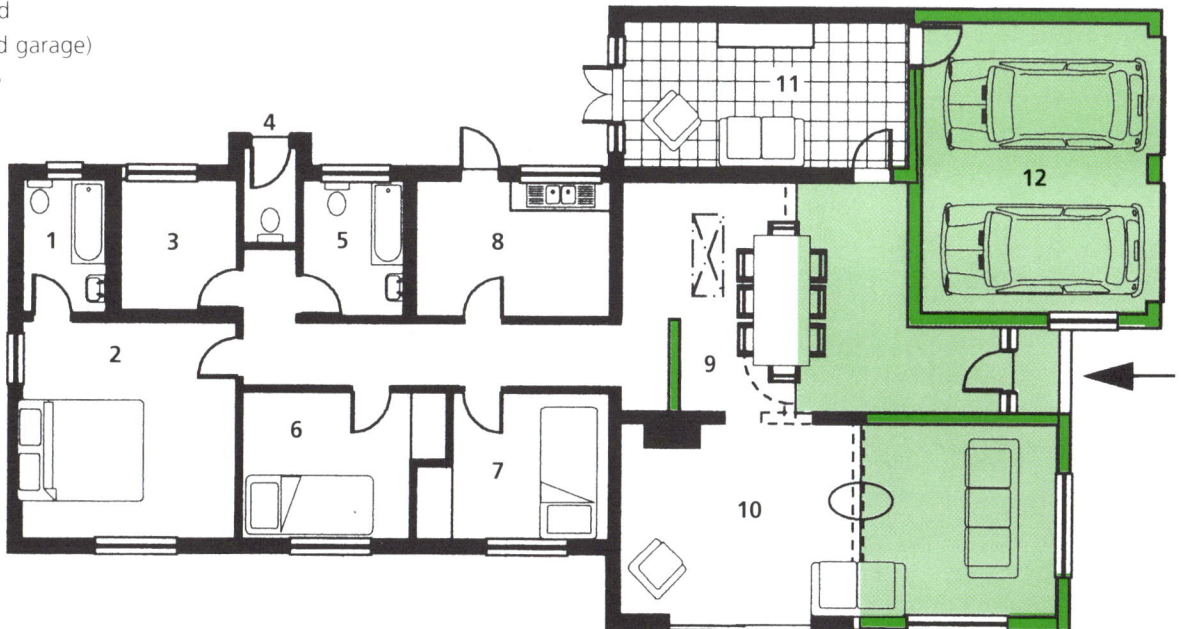

KITCHENS AND BATHROOMS

PLANNING

Planning extensions which include kitchens and bathrooms is a specialist task and many books have been dedicated to the design of these rooms. It is wise to think carefully about these spaces and look at books and magazines as well as your own and friends' kitchens and bathrooms to see if you can work out what you do and don't like. Do you like to eat in your kitchen? Or should it be tucked away and used only by staff? Do you like open-plan or closed rooms? Do you want an en-suite bathroom or would you prefer a large bathroom that can be used by the whole family? What are your needs for privacy from your children and guests?

ATTENTION TO DETAIL

Extensions to your home which include or make changes to kitchens and bathrooms require special attention to detail. Almost every building trade is involved in these extensions – plumbers, tilers, electricians and specialist joiners – and their co-ordination is essential. Consider and avoid detail problems such as:

- toilet-roll holders located behind toilets;
- towel rails positioned too far away from baths and basins;
- fridges, stoves and sinks located far from working spaces;
- having nowhere to put clothes when bathing;
- floor tiles that may cause you to slip when getting out of the bath or shower;
- lack of light over basins and work-tops; and
- no counter space to leave out items (toaster, kettle, etc.).

EXISTING SERVICES (WATER AND ELECTRICITY)

It is wise to inspect your property carefully and note the location of service points such as water supply, drainage and sewerage lines, and electricity boards. These will affect the siting of bathrooms and kitchens as these services can be co-ordinated. Moving manholes, electricity supply lines and other service lines can be costly. Sometimes it may be necessary to the plan the location of the extension on a side of the house which is not near services and the costs of moving these will need to be included in your budget.

DECIDE BEFORE YOU BUILD

Before any work is started on kitchen or bathroom extensions, you should ask an architect to draw large-scale plans detailing the layout, the location of all taps and drains, wall- and floor-tile layouts, and the location of electrical points.

This information should be discussed and confirmed with you, and shown to the builder before work begins on the extension. The cost of this work will need to budgeted and the information presented to the builder so that he has sufficient time to co-ordinate his subcontractors and staff.

PLANNING A KITCHEN

Most kitchen furniture ranges are manufactured in standard sizes: in metric measures of 500 to 600 mm for cupboard units and 600 mm depth for kitchen counters. The usual height of a kitchen counter is 900 mm from the floor. These dimensions can be altered if you need a purpose-built size and it is rare that the standard base units will fit exactly between the walls of a kitchen.

You can employ the services of specialist kitchen contractors who will help you plan your kitchen and draw the proposals. Alternatively, you can draw your own kitchen plan based on the existing kitchen and your preferences. Designing a kitchen is complicated as there are many factors that need to be taken into consideration.

WORKING WITH AN EXISTING KITCHEN

When working with an existing kitchen space, it makes economical sense to position fixtures and appliances as close as possible to the existing services, unless these locations have proved unsuccessful in the past.

Sinks and dishwashers need to be near the water supply, but if this means sacrificing a well-planned kitchen, it is wiser to pay for their relocation than to accept an inefficient arrangement. Any service changes need to be made before the furniture is added, as changes at a later stage will be costly. Consider adding electrical points above and below counter tops and at special heights to allow easy-access switching on and off for appliances such as dishwashers and fridges that require regular defrosting.

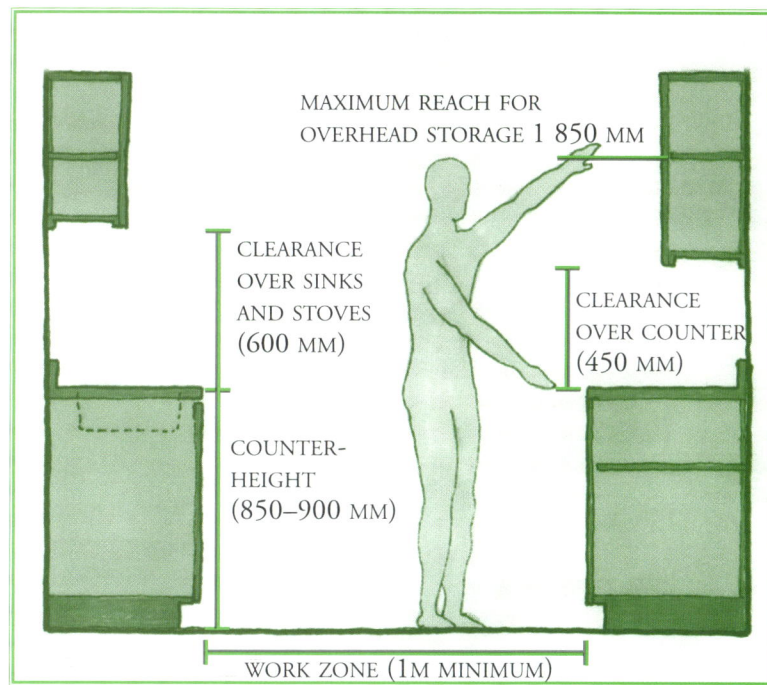

MAXIMUM REACH FOR
OVERHEAD STORAGE 1 850 MM

CLEARANCE
OVER SINKS
AND STOVES
(600 MM)

CLEARANCE
OVER COUNTER
(450 MM)

COUNTER-
HEIGHT
(850–900 MM)

WORK ZONE (1M MINIMUM)

RELOCATING A KITCHEN

Where it is not possible to enlarge an existing kitchen or when its location interferes with your ideas for extending your home to such a degree that relocation is essential, you will need to consider adding a new kitchen or adapting an existing room. What follows is a list of hints and tips for electrical, plumbing, flooring, cupboard and counter factors should relocation be a necessity.

Electrical

* Ensure there are more than enough carefully located and accessible plug points.
* Consider locating plug points under-counter for washing machines, dishwashers and tumble dryers, with the switches and taps located above-counter for easy access.
* Lighting should be bright and efficient so that you can see what you are doing on all the counters. Consider locating separate lights and switches under wall cupboards so that they shine onto the counters. The main light can be switched off in an open-plan kitchen to create a softer mood when preparation work is over.
* Check regulations for locating plug points near sinks.
* Consider the wall tiles you want to use above the counters in the kitchen as the plug points can be fitted in line with tile joints. This needs to be planned at an early stage as plug boxes need to be built into walls.
* Ask the electrician to provide a separate circuit for plugs in your kitchen as this is where electricity is usually in peak demand and you want to avoid the board tripping.
* Consider installing an extractor fan or an oven extractor to remove cooking smells.

Plumbing

* Ensure there is counter space on at least one side of your sink fitting.

* Consider locating taps for washing machines and dish-washers above-counter, in an accessible location, or check if your sink tap can have another tap attached to it.
* Consider locating a sink and dishwasher in a scullery area separate from the counters. You may want a separate laundry space for washing machines, washing sinks and tumble dryers.
* Consider using lever-handle mixer taps for sinks as these are easy to turn on and off.

Flooring

* Tile is usually long lasting, but can be hard to stand on for long periods and cold. Consider under-tile heating.
* Sheet floor finishes are easy to clean as there are few joints.
* Ensure that your floor finish is easy to clean and non-slip.

Cupboards and counter tops

Your choice of cupboards and counter tops will depend on your individual needs, taste and budget.

* The best counter top is usually granite, but it is expensive.
* The most popular counter-top finish is formica which comes in many different shades. It can be edged with wood or formica.
* Try well-sealed timber for a warm look, but consider adding granite or tile inlays for putting down hot pots.
* Cupboard fronts can be made to create a certain style or appearance.
* Whatever finish you choose for the doors and handles, ensure that the cupboards are well planned and offer you sufficient space for your needs.
* Consider deep drawers for heavy pots as these can be pulled out for easy access.
* Ensure that corner cupboards have doors designed to allow easy access.

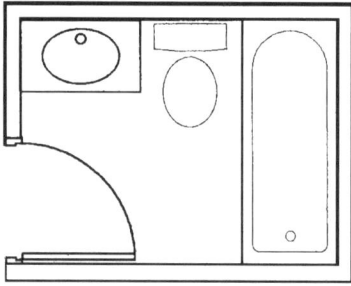

One-wall layout

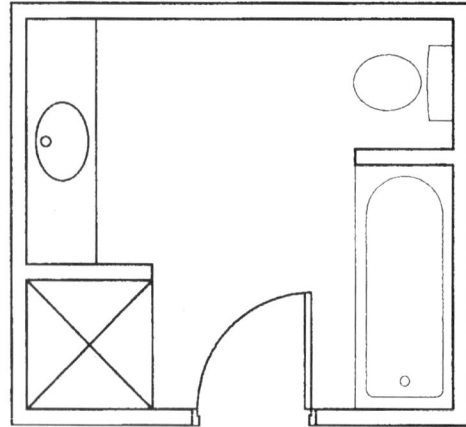

Using alcove spaces

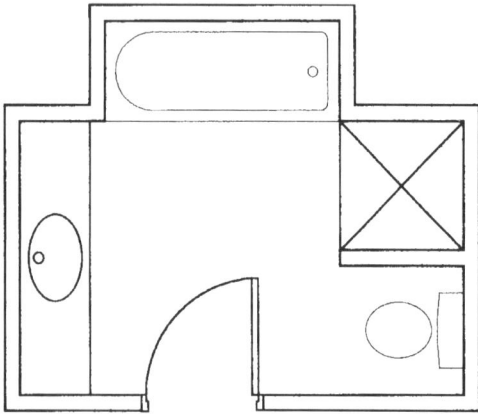

Two-wall layout

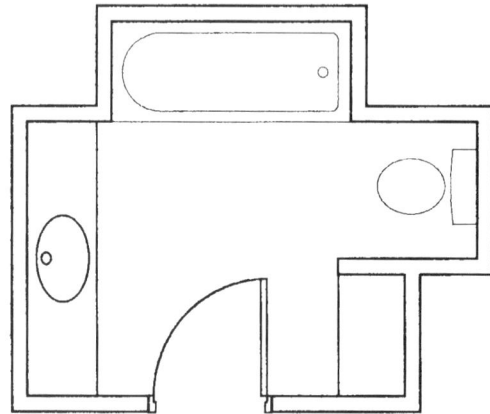

Compartmentalised bath

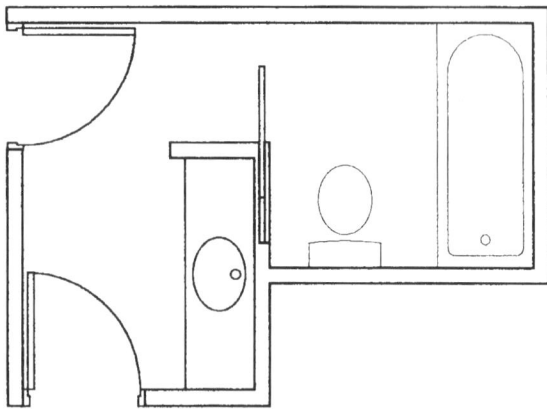

Three-wall layout

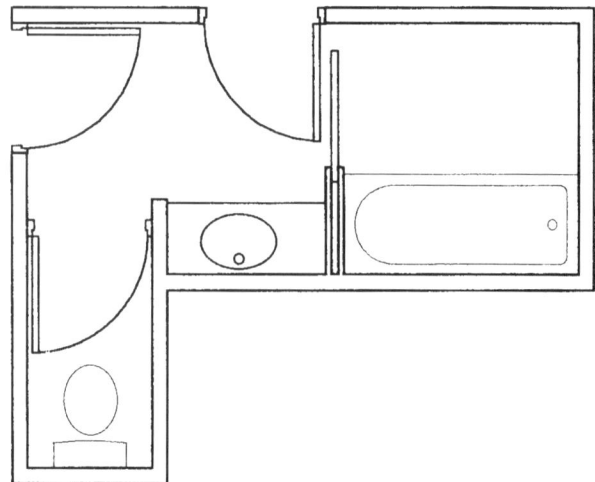

Compartmentalised bath and WC

PLANNING A BATHROOM

Bathrooms, like kitchens, are important features in a home and require special attention to detail and planning to look good and work well. Accessories such as toilet-roll holders and towel rails should be easily reached; there should be space for magazines and cosmetics. You may even want to include a space to sit or a jacuzzi so that family and friends can join you.

Not only is the layout of your bathroom important, its position in the house is critical. Some people like an en-suite bathroom from their bedrooms while others prefer the bathroom entrance to be in a lobby or passage. Ensure that an en-suite bathroom is not the only bathroom in the home, as children and guests will have to walk through the bedroom to get to it. If possible, have a full bathroom for general and guest use, with a separate toilet, and, if finance and space permits, consider an en-suite for the main bedroom.

It is best to locate bathrooms near bedrooms and position the doors away from living spaces. Privacy needs also differ. Some people are happy to have a bath located in a bedroom and a toilet is not something that needs to be invisible. Some prefer a large family bathroom into which people are welcome to walk in and out, while other people feel the need to have separate and private spaces for these facilities.

It is preferable to get lots of natural light and ventilation into a bathroom, but these rooms can often work internally with artificial light and extractor fan ventilation.

Consider the views from the bath or toilet to the outside and the creation of private gardens outside bathrooms so that windows near baths can be low. Consider the fittings you require in your bathroom – toilet, bath, shower, washbasin, bidet, etc. The positioning of these fittings is also critical. Try and keep all wet facilities, such as baths and showers, close together and not near the access doors. Think about which facilities you use most and make sure these are conveniently located.

Fitting heights are critical: washbasins need to be reached, baths need to be climbed into without great effort (beware of sunken baths as it is not easy to bath children in these).

Consider the accessories important to each facility and where they will be located. Baths need towel rails and shelves for soaps and oils; toilets need toilet-roll holders, cleaners, dustbins and possibly magazine shelves located nearby; washbasins need accessories for toothbrushes, mugs, cosmetics, mirrors (maybe mirrored cupboards).

The choice of finishes for the walls and floors are also important considerations. Floors can be:

- *Tiled.* Ensure that these are non-slip tiles and consider under-tile heating for winter.
- *Carpeted* – though preferably not in a childrenís bathroom. Ensure that the carpet is loose-laid with a rubber backing and that it can be washed.
- *Sheet flooring.* Cork or synthetic flooring can be warm underfoot, easy to clean and pleasant in appearance.

Bathroom walls are traditionally tiled, but not necessarily from floor to ceiling. It is sometimes possible to tile walls to a certain height only and add a timber rail at the top of the tiling height to add warmth and character. Wood panelling can also be used. Wallpaper in the form of photographs of family and friends, sealed with a polyurethane or other suitable finish, can also be considered. And with the many special paint effects available, the wall finish can really be left up to your imagination.

The bathroom addition in this project is part of a new upper floor extension which includes a dressing room and a bathroom. Features of this bathroom are the large skylight so that you can see the stars at night, when lying in the bath, and the triangular-shaped windows which create a shelf alongside the bath and magazine shelf near the toilet. The view from the toilet is over the garden towards mountains. It is not easy to see into this space from the outside.

The washbasin is located in a marble vanity top and toothbrushes and cosmetics are hidden from sight in a shallow, sliding-mirror cupboard above the vanity. The bath is surrounded by tiled shelves and the bath taps have been positioned on the outer side of the bath so that they are easily accessible.

Small square windows punctuate the walls above the triangular windows, giving this room an interesting and dynamic feel.

Towel rails are positioned near the bath and the wash-basin, and there are shelves where you need them for bath oils, magazines and other accessories related to this place of relaxation.

New upstairs plan

1. Balcony
2. Bedroom
3. Bathroom
4. Dressing room
5. Steps

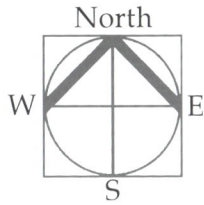

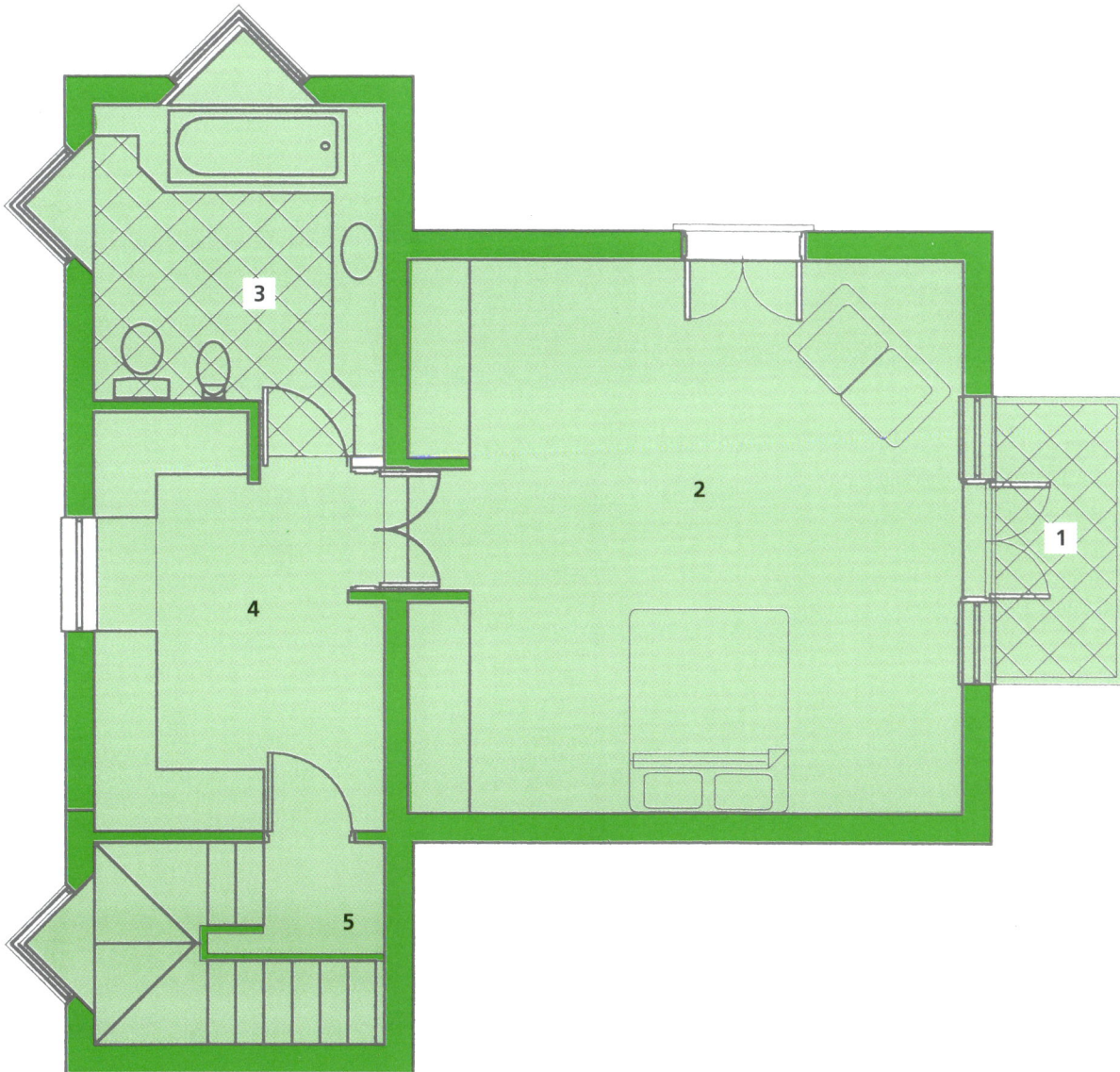

North

W   E

S

0m   1m   2m   3m   4m   5m

3

2

1

4

5

The changes to this home took place mostly at the back of the property with a kitchen redesign and a guest suite/study conversion.

A new sunny courtyard was created off the kitchen and the guest suite by demolishing a store outbuilding. A fountain water feature was added to the courtyard and positioned in line with the new kitchen's French doors.

One of the owners works from home and the altered study has an entrance off the courtyard so that people concerned with the business have an access separate from the main house. The house is located on a corner so there are two street accesses. This allows the separation of the space for public and private use. The study space could also be used for housing guests or for renting out.

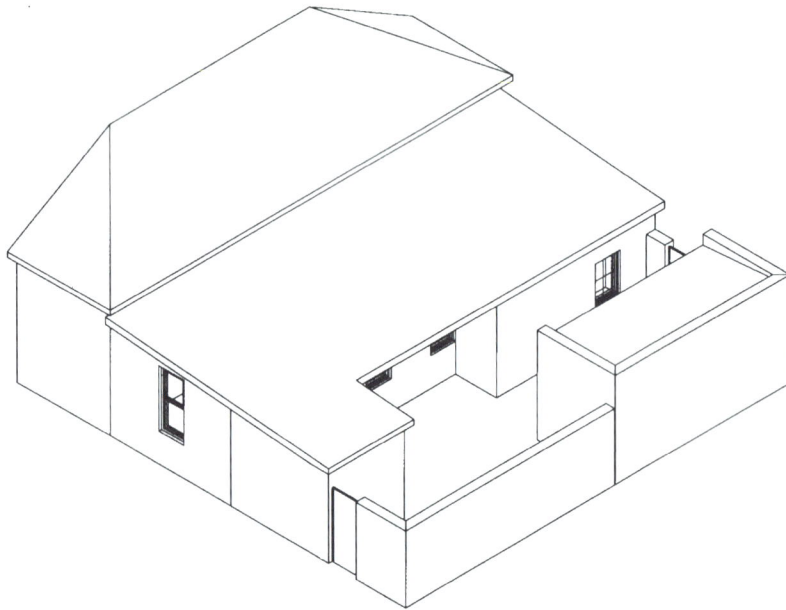

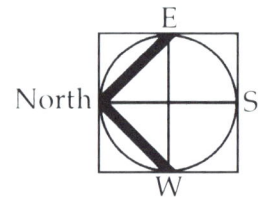

North E S W

0m 1m 2m 3m 4m 5m

Before part plan

1. Kitchen
2. Pantry
3. Bathroom
4. Bedroom
5. WC and shower
6. Store
7. Outside WC
8. Yard
9. Store room

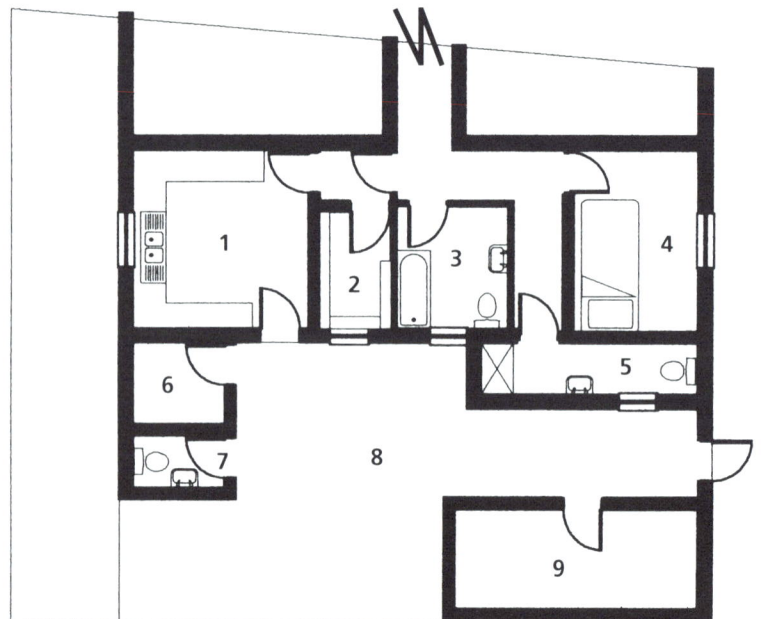

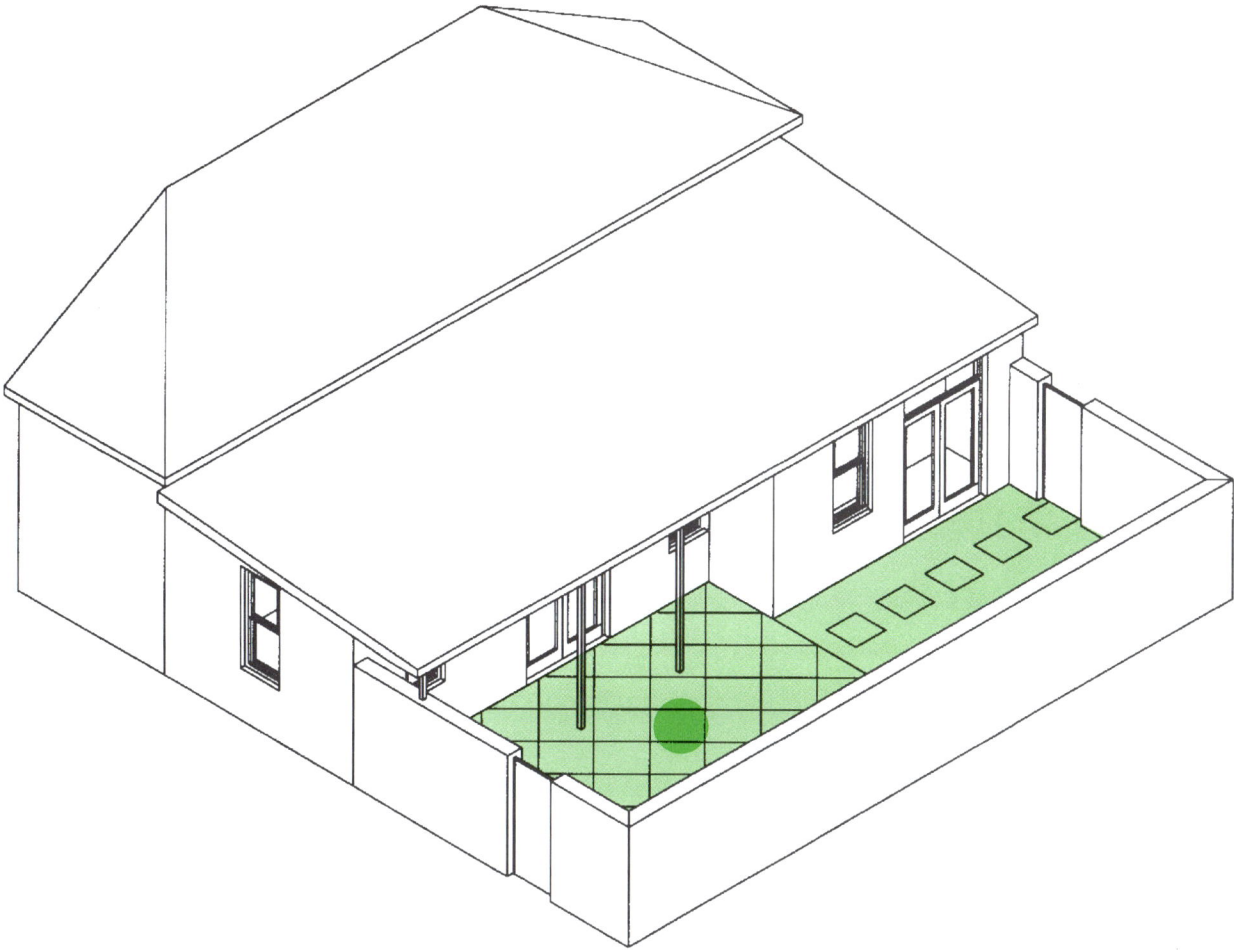

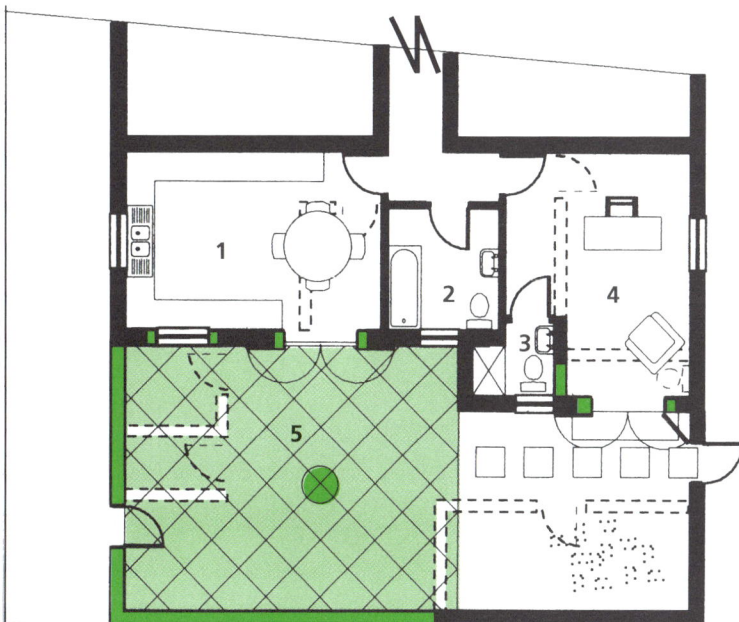

After part plan

1. Re-designed kitchen (pantry removed)
2. Bathroom
3. WC and shower
4. Study/office
5. Paved courtyard, with fountain, walls and gate

The original kitchen was extended into a larger live-in kitchen using a glazed conservatory-type structure which brings sun and light into this space and makes it feel part of the tree-filled garden. This sort of glazed extension is only suitable on the cooler sides of a home (preferably south-facing) as it can become very hot in summer. Even when such an extension is located on the south side, blinds and an extractor fan may still be required. It works well in this example because there are trees in the garden which create shade for the glazed roof.

Before plan (part)

1. Kitchen

W
S · North
E

0m 1m 2m 3m 4m 5m

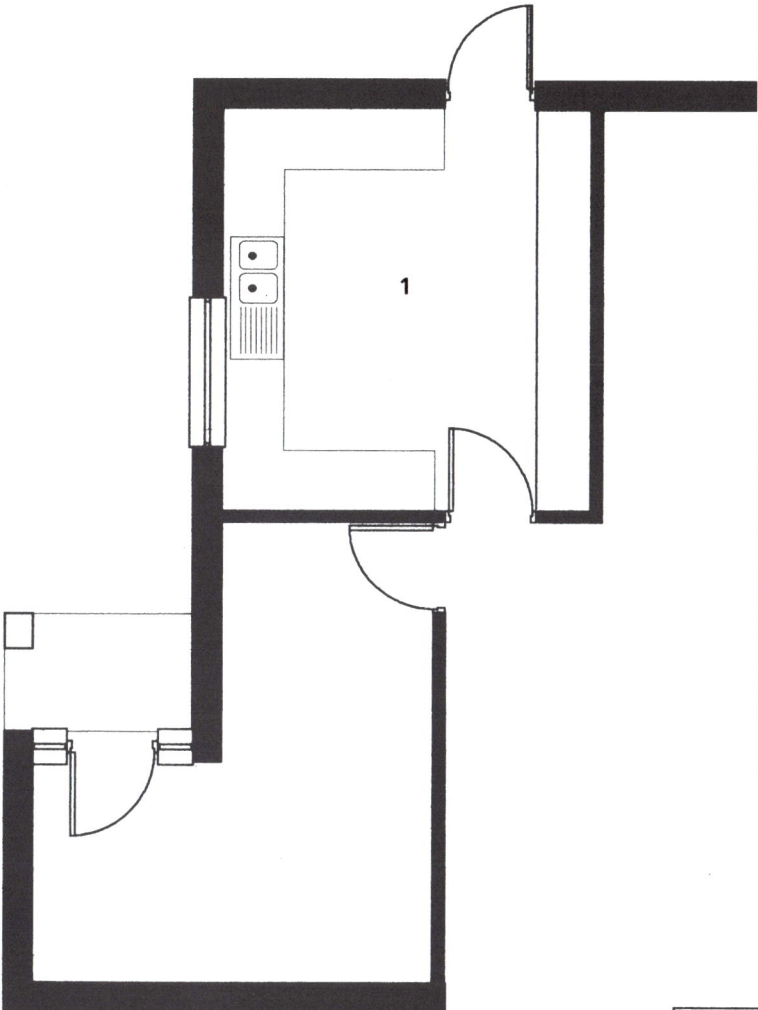

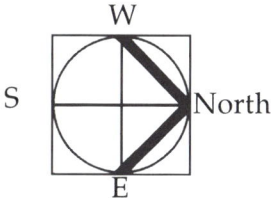

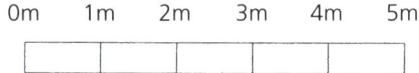

After plan (part)

1. Kitchen
2. Conservatory-type extension to kitchen

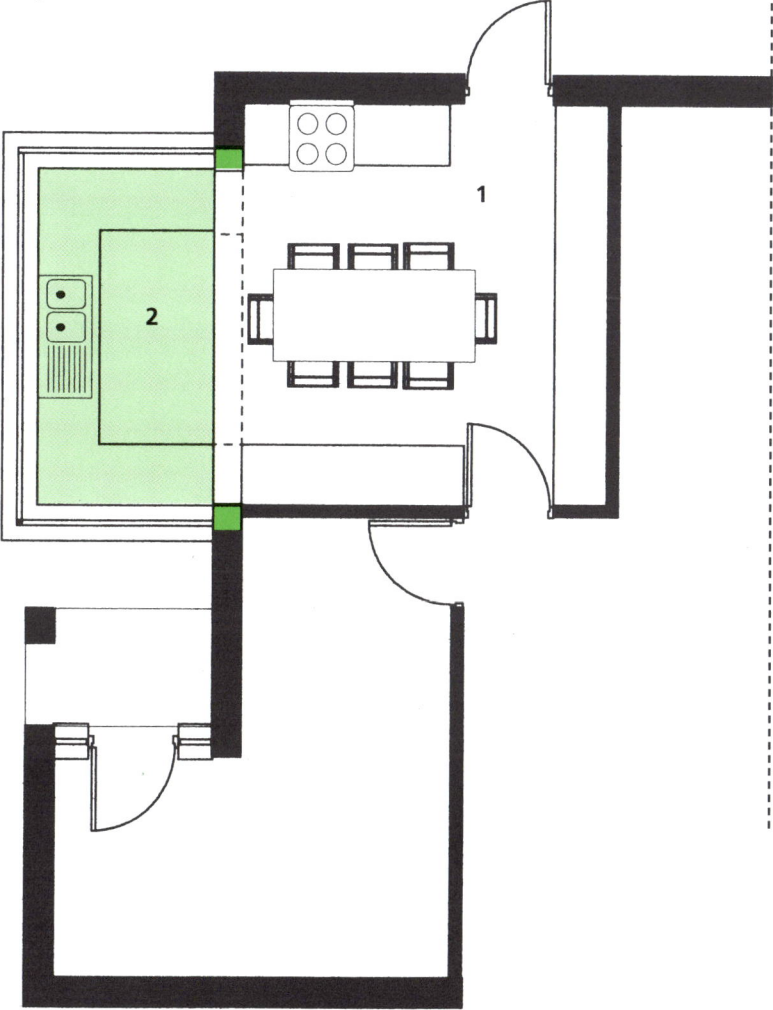

MINOR ADDITIONS

BAY WINDOWS

A bay window addition to a room is a simple way to make a space larger. It has the benefit of adding light from many sides and, if the ceiling of the bay window is kept lower than the main room ceiling, this space can be made to feel cosy and like another small room. Remember to add a light point and plug point in this space. There are many different ways of adding a bay window. The examples shown include:

• a bay window with a glazed roof;
• a bay window created simply by extending the main house roof;
• a traditional bay window with hipped roof and angled sides;
• a bay window with a simple, flat concrete roof (used when there is little headroom between the top of the window and the main house roof).

SKYLIGHTS

Skylights can be fixed or open, clear glazed or obscure glazed, depending on your requirements. They are simple ways to gain additional light in a dark room which faces the wrong direction and to gain sunlight. Skylights are easy to install and can have optional dome lights which link the opening in the roof to the ceiling via a foil tube. These fittings can be fitted by specialist supplier-installers in a day and the light from these skylights/rooflights can make an unbelievable difference to a room.

Consider adding blinds or shades to clear rooflights to block out sun. Beware of locating skylights on the west side of your house and in low ceilings as the space below can become very hot.

PATIOS

Patio extensions can make a living space larger and enhance the flow from inside to outside. They can be covered with roof sheeting or timber pergolas over which you can grow vines or plants.

Consider extending a tiled living room floor finish onto a new patio or using a similar finish so that the space between the interior/exterior flow together. Use glazed double doors between inside spaces and patios to allow in more light and create a larger opening to take tables and chairs out to the new patio.

ENTRANCE HALLS

The first space that you come to when you enter a home is often neglected. It is a very important transition area between the privacy of your home and the outside. It is the space where coats are hung, wet umbrellas are left, hellos and good-byes are said. You may want to locate your telephone in this space.

The impression of your home is gained from this one space. If you do not have the space for this important room, allow for a low wall to separate your front entrance from the immediate living area. A glazed screen may also be a suitable solution.

Simpler still – furnish the first room you enter so that a space is created around the front door separating it from the rest of the room.

DECKS

Usually crafted out of timber, decks tend to lend an air of relaxation to a home. Be sure to use the correct type of wood for a deck extension as it needs to weather without constant maintenance (although all exterior timber needs some kind of regular maintenance).

Speak to an architect or directly to decking specialists for advice on the type of timber and on the details for supporting and fixing the timbers and railings. A popular wood for decks is balua, but meranti can be used and teak (as a luxury) would be the best.

If stairs can be added from the deck to the garden, these can be built in timber or more solid material such as pre-cast concrete. Ensure that the deck fixings are rust-proof (brass, stainless steel or galvanised metal). The railing design can determine the style of the deck. You can use traditional, straight timber posts positioned approximately 125 mm apart (for child safety) or use diagonally laid cross members. If you live near the sea, consider using painted galvanised steel tubing or stainless steel cables. Steel or timber balustrades can be considered depending on the style of your home.

Building regulations call for a 1 m-high railing for a deck to prevent people from falling, but you may want an alternative such as a low-walled edge or space to grow plants .

FLAT-ROOFED BAY WINDOW

GLAZED-ROOFED BAY WINDOW

EXTENDED-ROOFED BAY WINDOW

TRADITIONAL HIPPED-ROOFED BAY WINDOW

A minor extension to this home created a glazed front porch. The front patio was tiled and seats were built into each side of the extension. The timber seat tops can be lifted so that outdoor furniture can be stored inside. With very little effort, this home gained another room leading to the garden and created an attractive entrance feature for the previously ordinary front facade.

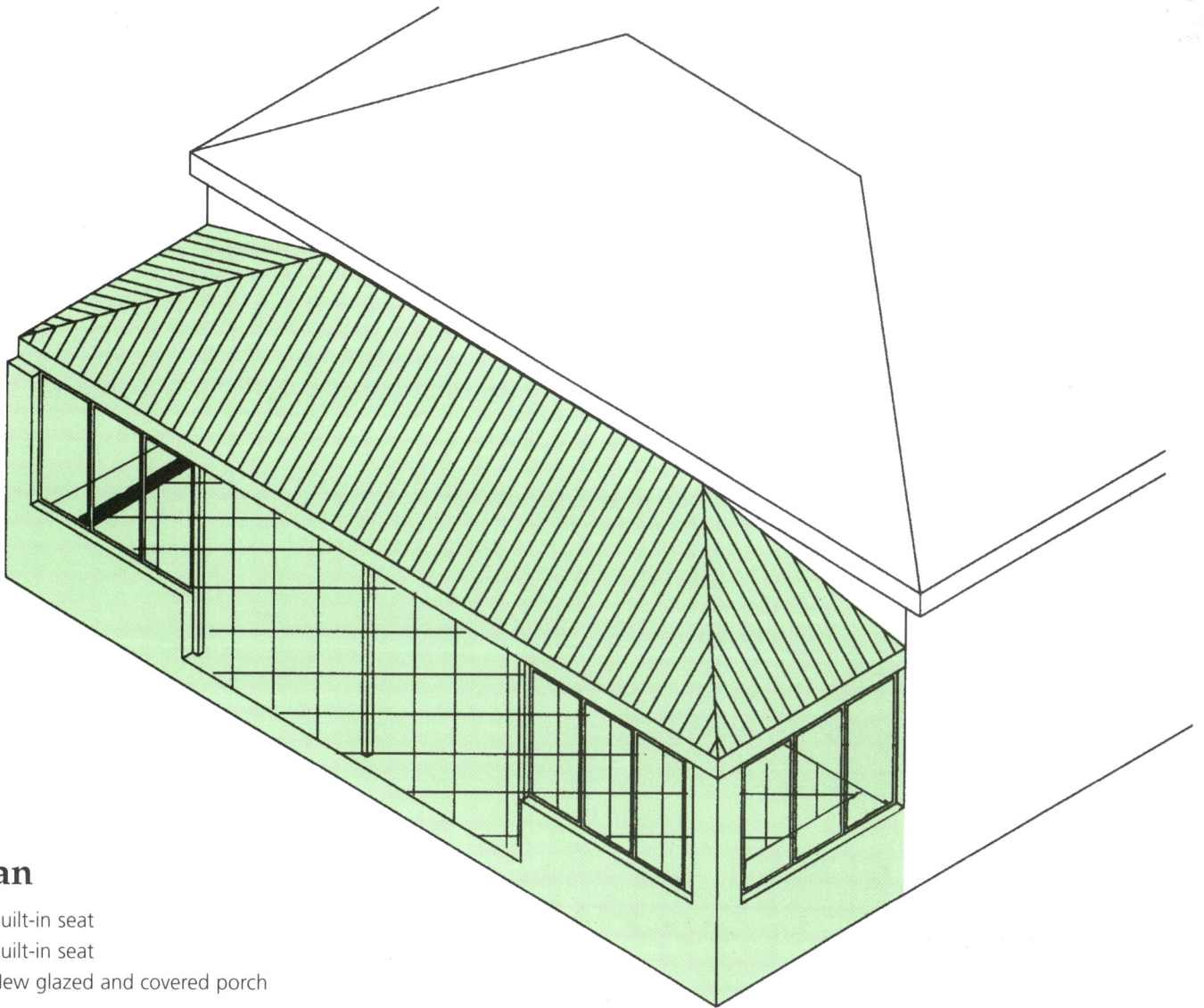

Plan

1a. Built-in seat
1b. Built-in seat
2. New glazed and covered porch

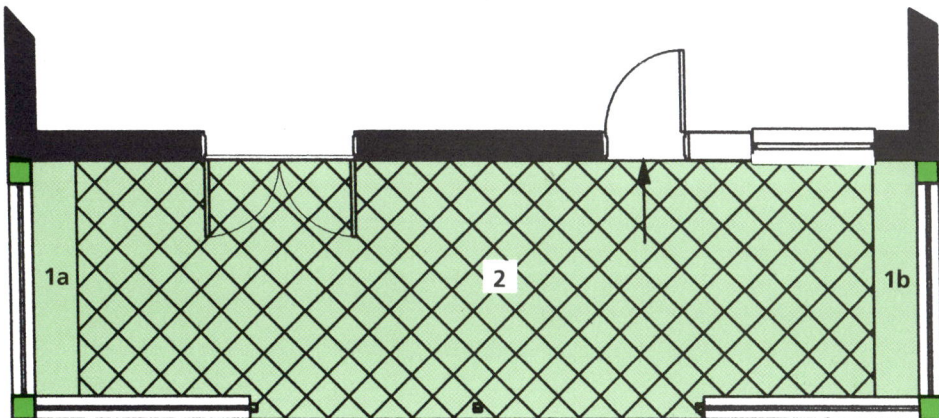

Several new facilities were added to this suburban home. A glazed entrance hall was created off the living room, facing the street entrance.

A new double garage with remote-controlled garage doors was built close to the street boundary. A lightly covered dining room courtyard now leads off the dining room and provides undercover access from the garage to the house. The existing entrance hall, originally located at the side of the house and not visible from the street entrance, was converted into a study. Patio and French doors lead off the bedroom spaces and give them access to the private back garden.

The dark facebrick chimney element was painted white along with the rest of the house and the timber windows and doors were treated. New entrance stairs with a timber rail lead from the new driveway, and the entrance path, pool surround and side patio were tiled with non-slip tiles to upgrade the house's exterior.

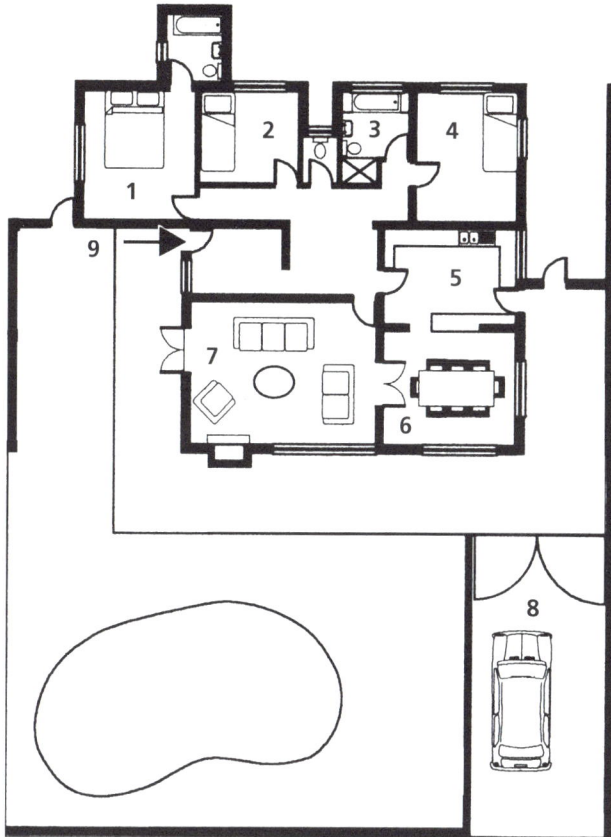

Before plan

1. Bedroom, with en-suite bathroom
2. Bedroom
3. Bathroom
4. Bedroom
5. Kitchen
6. Dining room
7. Living room
8. Carport
9. Entrance hall

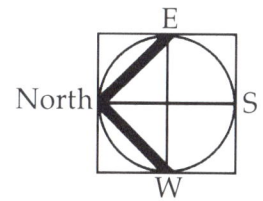

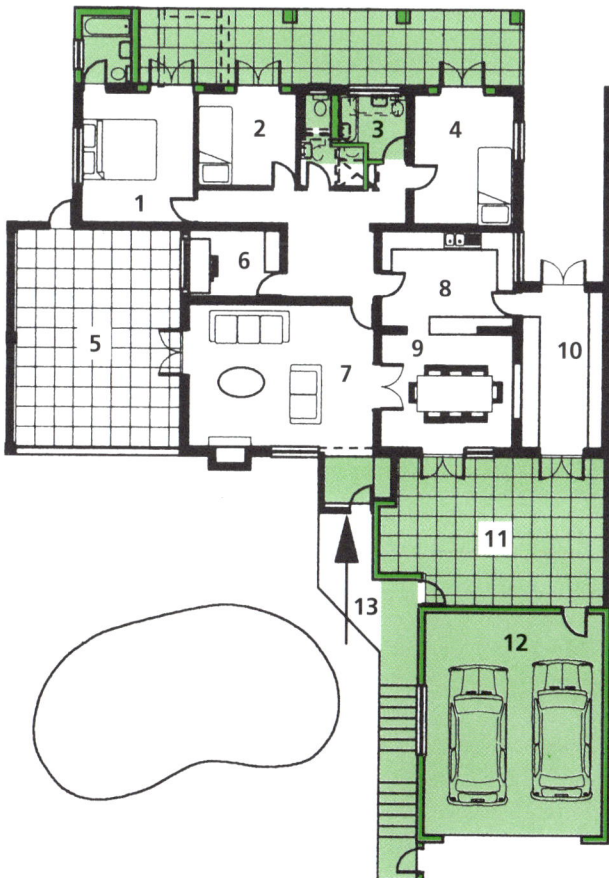

After plan

1. Bedroom, with en-suite bathroom
2. Bedroom
3. Bathroom
4. Bedroom
5. Patio
6. Study (converted entrance hall)
7. Living room
8. Kitchen
9. Dining room
10. Laundry
11. Covered courtyard, with built-in seat
12. Double garage
13. Glazed entrance and hall extension

0m 1m 2m 3m 4m 5m

North E S W

A modern stone cottage had the following features and spaces created: an entrance hall, a living room extension, a new patio leading off the living room, covered access from the new double carport to the new entrance hall, a timber deck leading off the attic room, the attic was extended and an en-suite bathroom installed. In this project the challenge was to match the extension finish with the original stonework. The roof also had a concrete shingle which needed to be matched. Dormer windows were added to bring light and ventilation to the new bathroom in the attic space, and a door was added from the attic bedroom leading out to a large timber deck. All the new doors and windows were made of matching timber to maintain the original style.

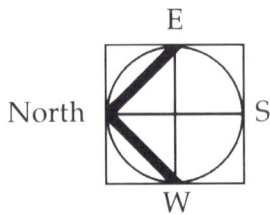

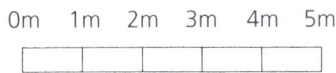

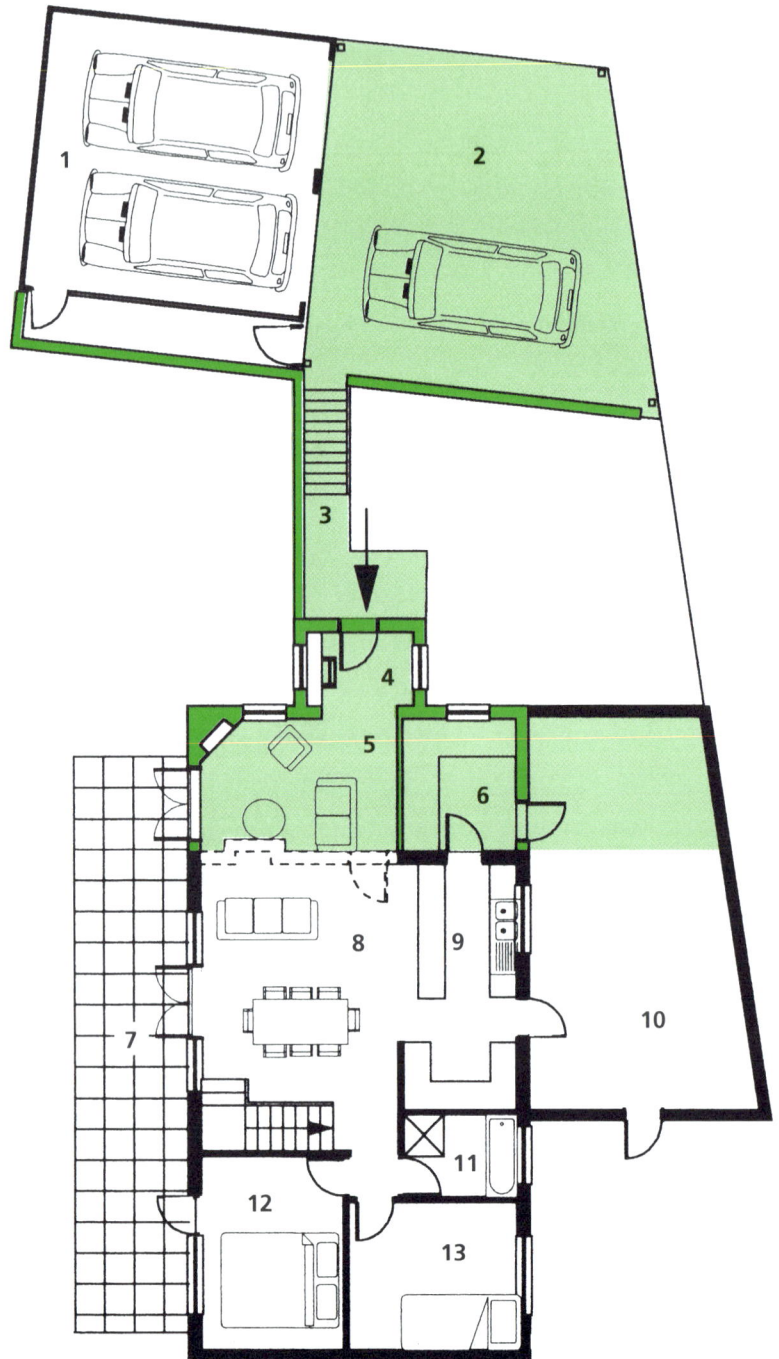

E

North   S

W

0m 1m 2m 3m 4m 5m

Plan

1. Double garage
2. Covered carport
3. Covered walkway and entrance patio
4. Entrance hall
5. Living room extension
6. Laundry
7. Patio
8. Dining/living area
9. Kitchen
10. Yard
11. Bathroom
12. Bedroom
13. Bedroom

A modern, three-storey-high house had its lower level converted into bedrooms so that the owners could be close to their young children and to stop toddlers from having to use the steps in the house.

The original lower-level space comprised a dark basement bedroom, a well-fitted study space, a small playroom and a bathroom with shower, toilet and washbasin. The converted area had its interior space rearranged to comprise a main bedroom with an en-suite bathroom and dressing room two extra bedrooms and a full bathroom. The original basement bedroom was enlarged by removing an unused store space and installing new doors and windows to the outside patio.

A bay window was added to the main bedroom to enlarge the space and gain views. The en-suite bathroom and dressing space were built in an unused courtyard.

Before plan

1. Courtyard unused
2. WC and shower
3. Bedroom
4. Study
5. Lower-level bedroom
6. Store
7. Lower-level patio
8. Patio

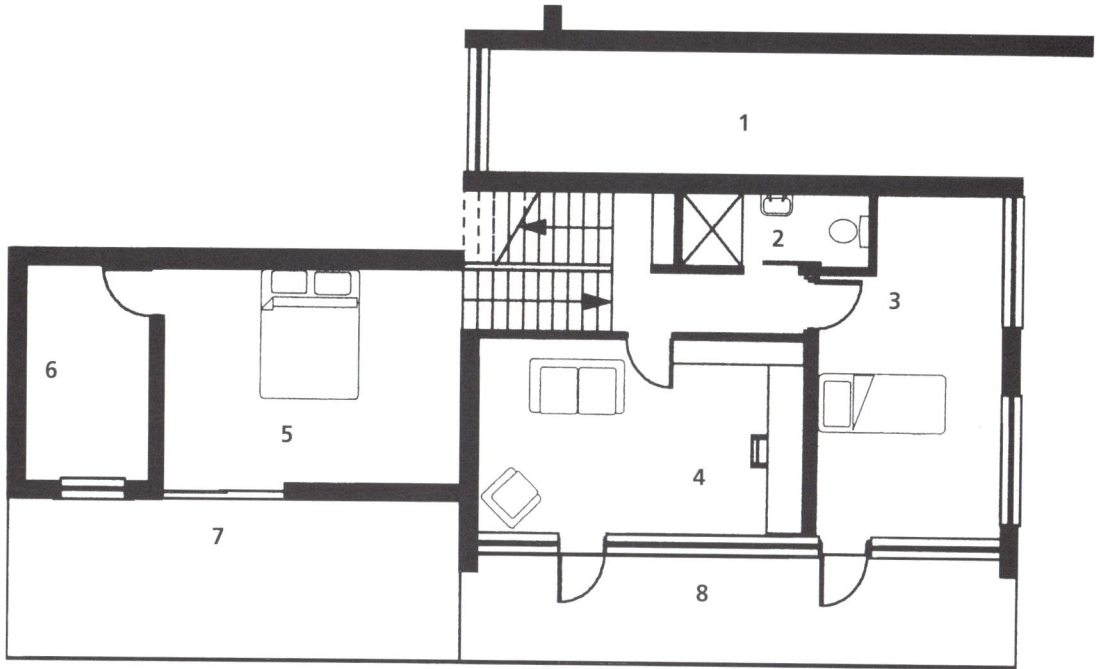

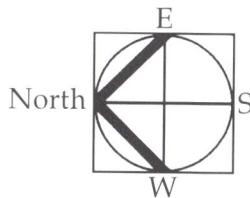

North E S W

0m 1m 2m 3m 4m 5m

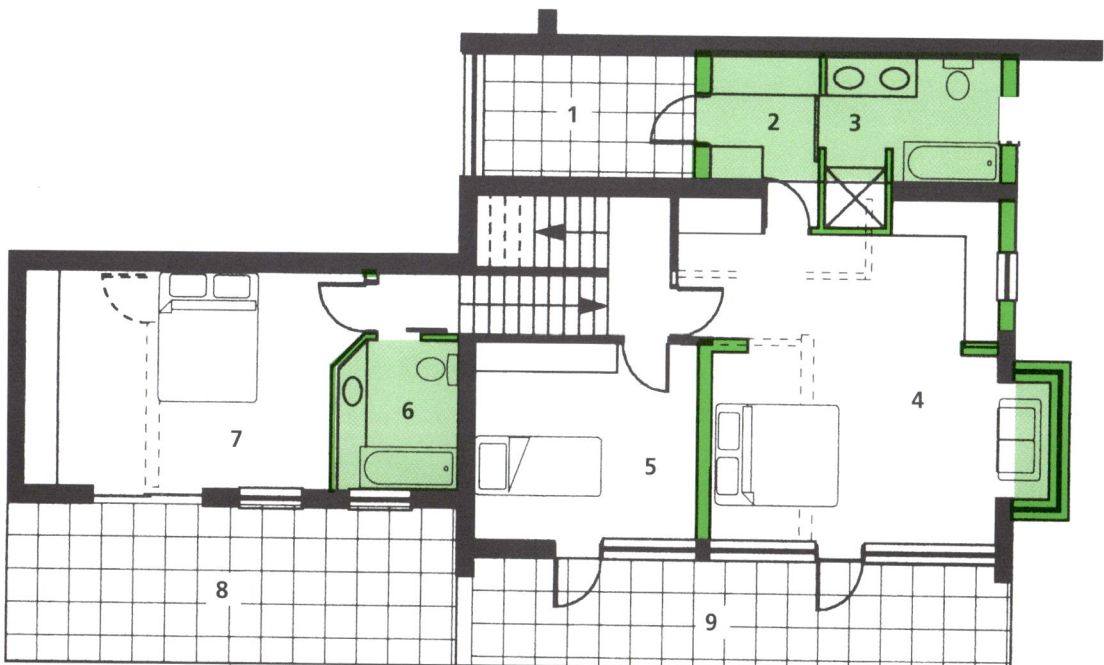

After plan

1. Courtyard reduced
2. Dressing room
3. Bathroom
4. Main bedroom, with bay window
5. Bedroom
6. Bathroom
7. Bedroom
8. Lower-level patio
9. Patio

PLAN SUMMARY

RE-ARRANGING SPACE	CONVERTING UNUSED SPACE	ADDING SPACE	BATHROOMS AND KITCHENS	MINOR ADDITIONS
Plan 1	Plan 9	Plan 1	Plan 2	Plan 2
Plan 2	Plan 10	Plan 3	Plan 4	Plan 3
Plan 3	Plan 11	Plan 5	Plan 5	Plan 25
Plan 4	Plan 12	Plan 6	Plan 7	Plan 26
Plan 5	Plan 13	Plan 7	Plan 8	Plan 27
Plan 6	Plan 14	Plan 8	Plan 10	Plan 28
Plan 7	Plan 15	Plan 13	Plan 11	Plan 29
Plan 8	Plan 16	Plan 16	Plan 12	Plan 30
Plan 11	Plan 18	Plan 17	Plan 13	Plan 31
Plan 12	Plan 21	Plan 19	Plan 14	
Plan 16	Plan 23	Plan 20	Plan 15	
Plan 17		Plan 21	Plan 16	
Plan 18		Plan 22	Plan 17	
Plan 21		Plan 23	Plan 18	
Plan 26		Plan 24	Plan 20	
Plan 29		Plan 29	Plan 21	
		Plan 30	Plan 25	
		Plan 31	Plan 26	
			Plan 27	
			Plan 31	

FURTHER READING

Before you Build, Habitat, 1983.

Brookes, John: *Room Outside*, Thames & Hudson, London, 1969.

Calloway, Stephen: *The Elements of Style*, Mitchell Beazley, London, 1991.

Conran, Terence: *The House Book*, Mitchell Beazley, London, 1974.

   Terence Conran's New House Book, Conran Octopus, London, 1985.

   The Kitchen Book, Mitchell Beazley, London, 1977.

Design Your Own Home, Struik, Cape Town, 1994.

Grobbelaar, Andre: *Home Planning and Building Guide*, Thompson Publications, Johannesburg, 1981.

Joyce, Peter & Hartdegen, Jacqueline and Paddy: *The Complete Book of Home Planning in South Africa*, Struik, Cape Town, 1991.

Reader's Digest Complete Guide to Home Improvements in South Africa, Reader's Digest, Cape Town.

Strauss, Pamela: *Africa Style in South Africa*, Jonathan Ball Publishers, Johannesburg, 1994.

Swift, Penny: *Bathrooms for the South African Home*, Struik, Cape Town 1988.

   Outdoor Style, Struik, Cape Town, 1993.

   The Complete South African House Book, Struik, Cape Town, 1991.

Swift, Penny & Goodbrand, Vaughan: *The Complete Book of Owner-Building in South Africa*, Struik, Cape Town, 1992.

The South African Book of House Plans, Struik, Cape Town, 1993.

GLOSSARY

Architect A person registered with the Institute of Architects, whose profession it is to design, specify and supervise buildings.

Building contract A contract signed by the property owner and the building contractor that confirms the cost of the building work, the time in which building is to take place, methods of payment, the roles of the parties involved in the contract and what to do if there are problems. The contract documentation can be supplied by Building or Architects' Institutes, be a specific contract issued by the builder, or be a contract agreed upon by the builder and the owner.

Joint Building Contract Committee (JBCC) Contract A building contract used mainly for large-scale building projects, but also suitable for smaller domestic contracts. It is used when an architect is appointed to act as the owner's agent.

Without Quantities Contract This is used for smaller domestic contracts, including new houses and extensions. It calls for a lump sum price from a builder and does not include a detailed cost breakdown, but a schedule of rates for the various building elements. The builder may be asked to issue a breakdown of costs to the owner, but is not obliged to do this.

With Quantities Contract This is used for large building contracts. It includes the services of a quantity surveyor who will prepare a bill of quantities and detail every aspect of the building.

Building contractor A builder registered with a recognised building institute who contracts for work by tender or negotiation. He manages the building process and either employs his staff or subcontracts staff to perform the building work for which he is ultimately responsible.

Building inspector A person employed by the local authority/council who can advise on legal requirements when submitting plans.

Building line The limit or boundary within which you may build on your property.

Building regulations National regulations which govern building standards.

Council approval It is necessary to obtain approval from the local authorities for the proposed building work according to national building regulations and town planning regulations. Drawings need to be prepared and submitted to the local authority for scrutiny and approval for most new buildings and changes to existing buildings.

Construction drawings Detailed drawings from which a builder can build. These include layout drawings, electrical layout drawings, window and door schedules, finishing schedules and detail drawings.

Designer (Building) A qualified practitioner and specialist in domestic architecture. Designs are limited to floor areas less than 500 m^2.

Draughtsman A person qualified in the art of preparing working drawings; usually employed by architects and building designers.

Electrical points An electrical layout drawing should indicate the exact location of: plug points, light fittings, light switches, telephone connections, geyser location, bells, television plugs, and the electrical meter or distribution board.

Finishes Finishes are the elements that go over the basic structure of a home extension. Floor finishes include tiles, timber and sheet flooring. Wall finishes include plaster and paint, face bricks and tiles.

On-site supervision/inspection This is usually performed by an architect or engineer. Site inspections are carried out during construction to make sure that the building work is being done according to the approved drawings and specifications on which the builder's price is based. If the building work is undertaken using a standard building contract, it also includes general financial control of the project.

Owner-builder A person who builds his or her own home for personal satisfaction or financial reasons.

Prime cost (PC) items Prime cost is an amount allowed in a building contract or specification for items selected by the owner – for example, light fittings, carpets, tiles, kitchen cupboards and counters, etc.

Provisional amounts These are amounts budgeted for in the architect's specifications for items which need to be designed and require the services of a specialist. They are usually separate from the builder's work and may include kitchen cupboards, built in cupboards, etc.